green press INITIATIVE

Nomad Press is committed to preserving ancient forests and natural resources. We elected to print *Explore Rocks and Minerals!* on 30% post consumer recycled paper, processed chlorine free. As a result, for this printing, we have saved:

8 Trees (40' tall and 6-8" diameter)
3,425 Gallons of Wastewater
3 million BTU's of Total Energy
217 Pounds of Solid Waste
759 Pounds of Greenhouse Gases

Nomad Press made this paper choice because our printer, Thomson-Shore, Inc., is a member of Green Press Initiative, a nonprofit program dedicated to supporting authors, publishers, and suppliers in their efforts to reduce their use of fiber obtained from endangered forests.

For more information, visit www.greenpressinitiative.org

Nomad Press
A division of Nomad Communications
10 9 8 7 6 5 4 3 2

This book was manufactured by Thomson-Shore, Inc., Dexter, Michigan, USA
Job #581239
ISBN: 978-1-934670-61-3

Illustrations by Bryan Stone
Educational Consultant, Marla Conn

Questions regarding the ordering of this book should be addressed to
Independent Publishers Group
814 N. Franklin St.
Chicago, IL 60610
www.ipgbook.com

Nomad Press
2456 Christian St.
White River Junction, VT 05001
www.nomadpress.net

MIX
Paper from responsible sources
FSC® C013483

Manufactured by Thomson-Shore, Dexter, MI (USA); RMA581RC239, April, 2012

CONTENTS

Titles in the **Explore Your World!** Series

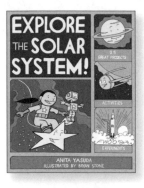

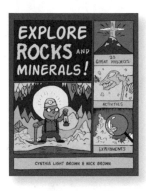

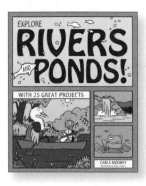

ROCKS ARE EVERYWHERE

Did you know that ROCKS and MINERALS are part of your life, every second of every minute of every day? Sound surprising?

Here are some ways and places to find rocks and minerals:

- Electricity runs through copper and aluminum wires
- Cars use steel, which is made from iron
- Houses use nails, bricks, and plaster, which all come from rocks
- Salt for seasoning food is a mineral
- Plants grow in soil, which forms from rocks
- Your bones are made mostly of a mineral called apatite
- Earth itself is one big ball of rocks

You stand on rocks, you consume rocks, and your home is built from rocks and powered by rocks. You even have rocks in the form of minerals inside you!

Those are some pretty good reasons to learn more about rocks and minerals. But the best reason of all is that rocks and minerals are fascinating. Rocks can slowly form over millions and millions of years, or be blasted from a volcano in an instant.

Rocks are like puzzles that can tell us about the earth's history. Right where you're standing, there may have once been an ocean. Maybe there was a volcano, or even a huge mountain chain as big as the **HIMALAYAS**. The rocks can give you clues about the past.

WORDS 2 KNOW

ROCKS: solid natural substances that are made up of minerals.

MINERALS: naturally occurring solids that almost always have a crystalline structure. Rocks are made of minerals.

HIMALAYAS: a mountain chain between India and Tibet. It contains the world's highest mountain, Mount Everest, which is 29,029 feet (8,848 meters) above sea level.

In this book, you'll learn all about minerals. You'll discover the different types of rocks and fossils, and how they form. You'll also learn more about the forces at work on our home planet, Earth. You'll get to explore all of these ideas with fun projects and activities.

Rocks and minerals are all around you, and each one has a story to tell. So get ready to rock and learn!

MANTLE

CORE

CRUST

THE EARTH

You touch it every day. You've spent your entire life on it. It's your home. We all live on a giant ball called planet Earth. But we only see what's on the very outside of the earth. The rest— the inside of the ball—is quite different. Even the outside shell of the earth where we live behaves differently than you might imagine!

No one has traveled to the center of the earth, but we know some things about what's inside. We know that there are layers that have different kinds of rocks. The three major layers are the **CRUST** on the outside, the **MANTLE** in the middle, and the **CORE** at the center. These layers probably formed as the earth itself was forming.

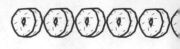
We also know that it gets hotter towards the center, and there is a lot more **PRESSURE.** This makes sense because pressure increases when there is a greater force pushing on something.

If you lie down on the floor and two friends lie on top of you, you will feel pressure from their weight. You will also feel hotter after a little bit, because pressure makes temperatures increase. The same is true for rocks closer to the center of the earth. They feel a LOT more pressure because of the weight of the rocks on them. They also have higher temperatures because of that pressure.

If you could travel to the center of the earth, what would you see?

WORDS 2 KNOW

CRUST: the thin, hard, outer layer of the earth.

MANTLE: the middle layer of the earth. Some areas of the mantle have melted rocks. It is soft enough that the rocks flow very slowly.

CORE: the center layer of the earth composed of iron and nickel. It has two parts: a solid inner core, and a liquid outer core.

PRESSURE: the force applied to something.

CONTINENTAL CRUST: the part of the earth's crust that forms the continents.

OCEANIC CRUST: the earth's crust under the oceans.

START AT THE CRUST

In your imaginary trip, you would start at the crust, which is the thin, hard outer layer of the earth. If you were standing on a continent, you would have to tunnel through crust anywhere from 16 to 56 miles thick (25 to 90 kilometers). That may sound like a lot, but compared to the rest of the earth, it isn't.

The rocks would look a lot like those on the surface. However, you might feel a bit warm, because they're about twice as hot as boiling water.

If you traveled to the center of the earth as fast as a car on the highway—55 miles per hour (89 kilometers per hour)—here's how long it would take to go through the layers:

Crust One hour
Mantle 32 more hours, or 33 hours total
Core 38 more hours, or 71 hours total

What's in Our Basement?

Very old rocks! The earth's **CONTINENTAL CRUST** has a basement, just like many houses do. The continents have very old rocks at their center, and geologists call them basement rocks. In most places, these old rocks are covered by younger rocks, but in some places they're exposed on the surface. The oldest rock found is over four billion years old! The crust under the oceans is about 20 times younger—less than 200 million years old. **OCEANIC CRUST** keeps getting recycled because of something called plate tectonics. You'll learn more about plate tectonics later in this chapter.

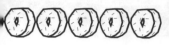 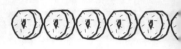
MANTLE IN THE MIDDLE

At the base of the crust, things would start to change. Better make sure you have some heat protection! The mantle is much hotter than the crust—about 1,000 degrees Fahrenheit (1,600 degrees Celsius) or more.

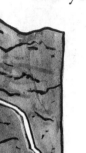

The rocks would start to look darker and they would be heavier. But they would also be softer, because it's so hot. Mantle rocks are a bit like Silly Putty, which gets softer if you squeeze it in your warm hands. The rocks are soft enough that they move around very slowly. In parts of the mantle, especially in the very upper mantle near the crust, the rocks are partly melted and move around more. The melted parts are called **MAGMA**.

Your trip through the mantle would be longer than through the crust, because the mantle is thicker—about 1,800 miles thick (2,970 kilometers).

WORDS 2 KNOW

MAGMA: molten rock.

COMPASS: an instrument used for navigation, with a needle that always points north.

MAGNET: a substance that attracts iron and produces a magnetic field.

MAGNETIC FIELD: a field of force produced by a magnetic object.

THE CORE OF THE MATTER

If you keep going, you'll come to the core of the earth. The outer core is so hot that it's liquid. The inner core is solid. All of the core is made of metal, mostly iron and some nickel. The core is the thickest layer of all—about 2,100 miles (3,400 kilometers) thick.

The inner core is about 7,000 degrees Fahrenheit (4,000 degrees Celsius). It might be even hotter. That's 20 times hotter than your oven when you bake cookies, and almost as hot as the surface of the sun!

But the inner core is solid. Don't things melt when they get hotter? They do, but the inner core also has enormous pressure on all sides from the weight of the earth. That much pressure keeps the inner core rocks from flowing. They're locked in place!

**THE SUN
(ABOUT 9900°F)**

A Giant Magnet

Have you ever used a **COMPASS**? The needle always points to the north. It works because the earth is a giant **MAGNET** and the compass needle is a small magnet, so it's controlled by the **MAGNETIC FIELD** of the earth. One end of the compass needle always points towards the North Pole and the other end points to the South Pole.

The earth is magnetic because its core has magnetic material (iron) that moves around and creates a giant magnetic field. A little piece of iron would be affected by the earth as far away as 37,000 miles (60,000 kilometers) in outer space. That's more than 5,000 times as high as a jet flies!

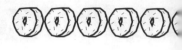

TRY THIS!

Ask an adult to hard boil an egg. Break the egg open. The shell of the egg compared to the whole egg is about as thick as the crust is to the whole earth. The white of the egg is like the mantle, and the yellow yolk is like the earth's core.

A PUZZLE THAT MOVES

The earth beneath your feet might seem solid, quiet, and unchanging. But things aren't always what they seem! In fact, the earth is always changing and moving, even if usually it's too slow for us to notice.

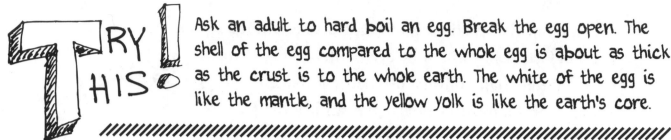

The earth's crust, along with the very upper part of the mantle, is actually broken into enormous pieces called **PLATES**. There are 12 huge plates, and several smaller ones. The plates fit together like a jigsaw puzzle. They are also constantly moving around, anywhere from 1 to 6 inches (2.5 to 15 centimeters) per year. The plates are a bit like solid rafts floating on the gooey mantle below them.

The plates move apart and bump against each other to produce earthquakes and volcanos and to build mountains. This is called **PLATE TECTONICS**.

WORDS 2 KNOW

PLATES: huge, interconnected slabs of the earth's crust that slowly move.

PLATE TECTONICS: the theory that describes how the plates move across the earth and interact with each other to produce earthquakes, volcanoes, and mountains.

GEOLOGISTS: scientists who study the rocks, minerals, and physical structure of an area.

METEORITE: a piece of rock that has entered the earth's **ATMOSPHERE**.

ATMOSPHERE: the gases that surround the earth.

How Do We Know About the Inside of the Earth?

No one has ever been to the center of the earth. Even just a few miles beneath the surface, the pressure is too great. The deepest hole ever drilled was in 1989 in Russia. It tunnels 7 miles (12 kilometers) below the surface. That's not even close to the bottom of the crust. So how do we know what the inside of the earth is like? **GEOLOGISTS** use information from many sources:

- Earthquakes make the ground vibrate in all directions. These vibrations are called seismic waves. Seismic waves can travel faster or slower and can change direction, depending on what kind of material they're traveling through. Geologists measure how long it takes these waves to travel through parts of the earth. Then they can figure out what some of the materials below the surface of the earth are, and where rocks are liquid or solid.

- There are some volcanic eruptions that bring up chunks from the mantle as deep as 93 miles (150 kilometers).

- Scientists run tests in the laboratory using very high temperatures and pressures similar to those deep in the earth.

- Scientists think that the earth was formed from the same material as **METEORITES**, so when meteorites fall to the earth, scientists analyze them.

The Earth Is a Giant Recycling Machine!

Earth has been recycling crust for a very long time—long before humans ever thought of recycling. New crust is formed where the plates move apart and magma rises. Think of the crust like a rigid board. When two plates move apart, the other end of each plate collides with other crust. At the collision, one plate is pushed under and melts. So the crust is created on one end, and destroyed on another. Eventually that melted crust will move through the mantle and become part of new crust. You can read about other ways the earth recycles rocks in Chapter 5, Metamorphic Rocks.

ON THE EDGE

EROSION, EARTHQUAKES, VOLCANOES, and mountains all happen where they do because of the movement of the earth's plates. That's because most of the action happens at plate boundaries where one plate meets another. There are three different kinds of plate boundaries.

BOUNDARIES WHERE PLATES PULL APART Hot magma rises from the mantle, and when it reaches the crust, it causes the plates above to move apart. The rising magma pushes out through the openings, and cools and hardens to form new rocks. New crust is being made! Nearly all of the earth's new crust forms at these boundaries, and most of them are under the ocean.

Sometimes when the plates keep pulling apart in a continent, it pulls apart so much that a shallow ocean forms. Geologists think that's what is happening right now in the Red Sea along East Africa. They think it will eventually become a major ocean.

BOUNDARIES WHERE PLATES SMASH TOGETHER

What happens when two plates smash together? That depends on what kind of crust the plates are made of. Oceanic crust is **DENSER** and thinner than continental crust. When an oceanic plate and a continental plate collide, the oceanic plate goes underneath the continental plate because it is denser. Volcanoes often erupt around these colliding boundaries. If continental crust collides with continental crust, then they both buckle upwards, forming mountains.

WORDS 2 KNOW

EROSION: the process where rocks are broken down by wind, water, ice, and gravity, and then carried away.

EARTHQUAKE: a shaking of the earth's crust because of movement in the earth's plates or because of a volcano's activity.

VOLCANO: an opening in the earth's crust. Magma, ash, and gases erupt out of volcanos.

DENSER: more matter in the same amount of space.

Did U Know?

Columbus Sailed Almost All of the Ocean Blue!

Columbus sailed the ocean blue in 1492, but he had it easy. He traveled about 33 feet less than he would if he traveled today, because the Atlantic Ocean is spreading apart at about 1/2 to one inch per year. So, there's about 33 feet in the middle of the Atlantic Ocean that Columbus never traveled over!

BOUNDARIES WHERE PLATES MOVE PAST EACH OTHER

Sometimes plates grind against each other as they move side by side. As the plates move past each other they sometimes rapidly slip. When this happens, it releases a huge amount of energy and gives a big lurch. That lurch is an earthquake! California has earthquakes because plates are moving past each other in this way.

BIRTH OF AN IDEA

Alfred Lothar Wegener, a German explorer trained as an astronomer, first developed the theory of **CONTINENTAL DRIFT**. He said that all of the continents had been joined together at one time. He didn't know how or why the continents had drifted, but he saw how the continents fit together almost like puzzle pieces. When he made a presentation about his theories in 1923, though, some other geologists thought he was crazy.

The top of Mount Everest isn't the point farthest from the center of the earth.

Because of its spinning, the earth actually bulges outward a bit (about 26 miles, or 43 kilometers) at the **EQUATOR** compared with the North and South Poles. Chimborazo Peak in Ecuador is only 7,113 feet (2,168 meters) above sea level, but it's the furthest point from the center of the earth because it's located close to the bulging equator.

Did U Know?

Then, in 1960, Harry Hess suggested that the ocean floors aren't permanent. He said that the ocean floors are spreading out from the middle, and at their edges the ocean crust is dragged down into the mantle. This would also cause the continents to move.

Mt. Everest is the highest point above sea level on Earth at 29,028 feet (8,848 meters). It sits on the border of Nepal and Tibet, China in the Himalaya Mountains. The reason it's there is because two continental plates are crunching together. And it's still rising about one centimeter every year, because the plates are still slamming together!

At first, other geologists were skeptical. But then they found some evidence under the ocean. Ridges of raised rock run down the centers of the oceans. Scientists found that on both sides of the ridges, the rocks became older the farther away from the ridges they went. Over time, other scientists gathered more evidence for the theory of plate tectonics. It took more than half a century, but Alfred Wegener was finally proved right!

WORDS 2 KNOW

CONTINENTAL DRIFT: the theory that all of the continents were joined together at one time and have since moved apart.

EQUATOR: the imaginary line dividing the north and south halves of the earth.

Ready, Set, Drift!

Most of the tectonic plates move at about ½–1 inch (1–2 centimeters) per year. Australia is a speed demon, though. It's moving north over 6 inches (15 centimeters) each year!

MAKE YOUR OWN EARTH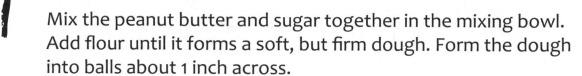

1 Mix the peanut butter and sugar together in the mixing bowl. Add flour until it forms a soft, but firm dough. Form the dough into balls about 1 inch across.

2 Cut the balls in half and scoop out the center of each half. Using the knife, fill the holes with jam, and place a chocolate chip in one half of each of the balls. Then put the two halves back together.

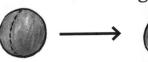

3 With an adult's help, melt the remaining chocolate in the microwave. Remove the bowl from the microwave using potholders. Roll the balls in the chocolate and place them on the wax paper—**be careful, the chocolate is HOT!**

4 Roll the balls in the coconut. Cut one open to look at your layers, and . . . yum! Who knew the earth could taste so good?

coconut

SUPPLIES:

- mixing bowl and spoon
- 1 cup peanut butter
- 1 cup sugar
- flour, as needed
- butter knife
- jam
- ½ cup chocolate chips
- microwave-safe bowl
- microwave oven
- potholders
- wax paper
- shredded coconut

WHAT'S HAPPENING?

The earth is composed of layers. Here's what your concoction represents:

Chocolate chip = *Inner, solid core*
Jam = *Outer, liquid core*
Peanut Butter Mixture = *Mantle*
Outer Chocolate Layer = *Crust*
Coconut = *Soil and plants*

MINERALS AND CRYSTALS

Have you ever picked up a rock and seen little specks sparkling in the sunlight? You were probably seeing minerals. Minerals can be so small you can't see them, or as big as a tree trunk. They can be almost any color you can imagine. Minerals are solid, natural SUBSTANCES that all rocks are made of. Almost all minerals form as CRYSTALS.

If you pick up a round, smooth pebble, you might think that there is no way that minerals are made of crystals. Crystals have edges, right? True, but even pebbles are made of **CRYSTALLINE** minerals. The crystals are just too small for you to see them. Or the rock might have bounced around in a river or the wind, which smoothed over the rough edges of the crystals.

WORDS 2 KNOW

SUBSTANCE: a kind of matter or material.

CRYSTAL: a solid with a definite geometric shape. Crystals have edges and smooth flat areas called faces. Crystals are made of atoms arranged in a pattern.

CRYSTALLINE: any material that has atoms arranged in a pattern that repeats itself. Minerals are crystalline materials.

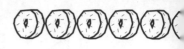

What makes one mineral different from another? To understand that, you have to know a little about the **ATOMS** that make up minerals. And you have to know how those atoms are arranged.

THE KINDS OF ATOMS

Everything in the **UNIVERSE** is made up of tiny particles called atoms. You're made of atoms, the air is made of atoms, and the sun is made of atoms. So are rocks and minerals. There are about 90 kinds of atoms that occur in nature, and everything in the universe is made of some combination of these atoms.

Different minerals are made of different kinds of atoms. The mineral gold is made of only gold atoms. The mineral quartz is made of **OXYGEN** and **SILICON** atoms. But what kind of atoms a mineral is made of is just part of what makes it unique . . .

Same Pattern, Different Atoms

Everyone is familiar with salt. It's white and, of course, it tastes salty. You probably have some in your kitchen. Gold is used in jewelry and is very valuable because of its beautiful color and shine, and the way it can be molded into interesting shapes. Although these two minerals are very different in how they look and feel, their atoms are arranged in the same pattern: a cube! The difference between gold and salt is that gold is made up of gold atoms and salt is made up of **SODIUM** and **CHLORINE** atoms.

HOW THE ATOMS ARE ARRANGED

If you could explore the inside of a mineral and see its atoms, you would see that the atoms are held together in patterns. The pattern could be in the shape of a cube, a **HEXAGON**, or another shape. Geologists classify those patterns into six different groups depending on their shape. The pattern of atoms is repeated over and over again to build a crystal.

In fact, that is what a crystal is: a substance made of atoms in a pattern. Sometimes the pattern only repeats enough to form a very small crystal, but often the pattern repeats enough to form a crystal big enough that you can see it. A mineral is the same all the way through. You can find the same pattern of atoms everywhere.

WOW!

Throughout the ages, many people have thought that gold is related to the sun, and silver is related to the moon.

WORDS 2 KNOW

ATOMS: the smallest particles that cannot be easily broken down.

UNIVERSE: everything that exists, everywhere.

OXYGEN: the most abundant element in the earth's crust. Found in air, water, and many rocks.

SILICON: the next most abundant element in the earth's crust. Found in sand, clay, and quartz.

SODIUM: a type of atom that combines with chlorine to form salt.

CHLORINE: a type of atom that combines with sodium to form salt.

HEXAGON: a shape with six sides.

Same Atoms, Different Pattern

You might have seen a diamond in a wedding ring or other jewelry. Diamonds are valuable because they are beautiful, rare, and very hard. In fact, they're the hardest natural substance on Earth! The reason they are so hard is because their atoms are packed closely together.

You've also seen graphite, which is used as the "lead" in pencils. Graphite is gray and smudgy looking. The reason graphite works for writing is that it is so soft that some of it rubs off on paper to make a mark.

It's hard to imagine two substances more different than diamonds and graphite. Here's the surprise: diamonds and graphite are made of exactly the same stuff—**CARBON** atoms! The only difference between diamonds and graphite is the pattern the carbon atoms are arranged in.

HOW DO CRYSTALS GROW?

Minerals, which are almost always crystalline materials, grow layer by layer. They form when a liquid cools and the atoms arrange themselves into a solid crystal pattern. Crystals need three things to grow: space, raw materials, and time.

Imagine you are arranging red and blue beads in a pattern on a piece of paper. You're using a simple pattern of red-blue-red-blue. If you fill up the paper, you will have to stop because you've run out of space. Crystals often grow in cracks, and they can run out of space to grow.

WORDS 2 KNOW

CARBON: a type of atom that is present in all life. It is what the minerals diamond and graphite are made of.

HABIT: the shape that a crystal tends to grow in.

You could also run out of blue beads and only have red left, which would change your pattern. Then you've run out of raw materials. Sometimes when crystals grow, they run out of a type of raw material, or atom, so that kind of crystal no longer grows—a different one does.

RAN OUT OF
BLUE BEADS

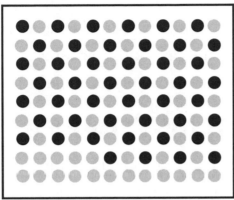

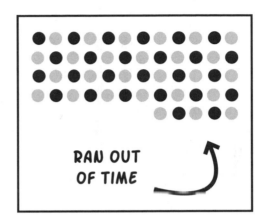

RAN OUT
OF TIME

Everybody Has Habits

Everyone has habits, and so do minerals. The shape that a mineral's crystals tend to grow in is called the crystal's **HABIT**. A crystal can grow in a blocky shape, or as thin, flaky sheets, or as needles. Its habits can change if the conditions change, just like your habits can change. You might brush your teeth every night. But maybe you have a sleepover one night and forget your toothbrush, or maybe your dog thinks your toothbrush is a chew toy!

Crystals are the same way. Something might come along to change the way the crystal usually grows, so that it forms a different shape. For example, crystals often grow in cracks, where they're closed in on different sides. When crystals are closed in on all sides as they grow, their natural shape is distorted.

19

The Kohinoor diamond in Great Britain's Crown Jewels was once known as the largest diamond in the world. It is 105 **CARATS**, the size of a small hen's egg, and its name means "mountain of light."

Finally, your mom could call you for dinner, and you would have to stop because you've run out of time. Crystals can run out of time too. They keep adding layers as long as the liquid is hot enough that the atoms can still move around and arrange themselves. But when a substance cools, the atoms can't move around as easily, and everything is set in place. Time's up!

GEMSTONES

GEMSTONES are minerals that are especially beautiful, durable, and rare. They often have a bright, vivid color and sparkle. Gemstones are usually cut or polished to show off their beauty.

Some gems, like opal or jade, are polished or carved. Other gems are cut to show flat surfaces, or **FACETS**. This causes the gem to reflect light and sparkle so brightly that it almost looks like it's on fire! Getting the right cut can be a tricky process. Diamonds are often cut with what is called the brilliant cut, which has a total of 58 different facets. Some of the most valuable gems are diamonds, emeralds, rubies, and sapphires.

The Hope Diamond is perhaps the most famous diamond in the world. It was found in India, and is now on display at the Smithsonian Museum in Washington, D.C. The Hope Diamond is unusual because it is blue, a rare color for a diamond. It has mysteriously vanished and been found again more than once!

Birthstones

Since ancient times and in many cultures, different gemstones have been associated with the months of the year that someone is born in. Here are the birthstones in the United States.

Red diamonds are the most expensive gems in the world.

- January–Garnet
- February–Amethyst
- March–Aquamarine
- April–Diamond
- May–Emerald
- June–Pearl
- July–Ruby
- August–Peridot
- September–Sapphire
- October–Opal
- November–Topaz
- December–Turquoise

How do you cut a diamond, the hardest substance on Earth? With another diamond of course! Diamonds can't be scratched, but they do have planes of weakness, and can be cut by powdered diamonds. Corundum is the second-hardest mineral, after diamond. It's found in many different colors. Red corundum is known as ruby, while its other colors are sapphires.

Gems have been used in jewelry for thousands of years. Gemstone jewelry was found in the tomb of Tutankhamun, an Egyptian pharaoh who ruled over 3000 years ago!

WORDS 2 KNOW

CARAT: a measure of weight for gems equal to 200 milligrams.

GEMSTONE: a cut or polished mineral that is beautiful, durable, and rare.

FACET: a smooth, flat, cut or polished side of a gemstone.

If you jump or dive deep into a pool, you can feel the increased pressure of the water on your ears. And the deeper you go, the more pressure there is. If you could go 90 miles below the surface of the earth, where diamonds form, you would feel about 50,000 times more pressure. Diamonds can only form where the pressure is very great, because their atoms have to be packed so tightly together.

If diamonds are created 90 miles below the earth's surface, how do we find them? They are often blasted to the surface in a volcanic eruption.

Did U Know?

COMMON MINERALS

You'll hear more about some of these minerals later in the book, because they form many rocks.

QUARTZ is the single most common mineral in the crust of the earth. It comes in a huge variety of colors and is found is many different kinds of rocks. Some varieties of quartz, like the purple variety called amethyst, are valued as gemstones.

FELDSPAR is really a group of minerals that make up about two-thirds of the earth's crust. They can be found in many different kinds of rocks, especially rocks like granite. If you took a trip to the moon, or a passing meteorite, you would find feldspars! They are usually off-white or pink, but can be other colors as well, like green or gray.

!WOW!

In ancient times, people thought quartz was ice that had frozen so hard it wouldn't melt.

MICA is another group of minerals. It can be almost black or so clear you can see right through it. Micas have a crystal habit that is flat, and they can be split into thin layers. Before people knew how to make clear glass, mica was sometimes used as "glass" in windows. In fact, it is still used in the windows of some stoves because it doesn't break easily at very high temperatures.

OLIVINE is one of the most common minerals on Earth, so you might expect that it would be easy to find. Nope! It lies in the mantle of the earth, deep below the surface. It also exists in the tails of comets, on Mars, the moon, meteorites, and in the dust around stars. One place it's easier to find is in some volcanic rocks like basalt. In most basalt, however, the grains are too small to see with just your eyes. Rare, transparent crystals of olivine are the beautiful gem called peridot. Olivine's color? Just what you would expect—olive green!

Mica is also used in hair dryers and irons because it is resistant to heat. When it's ground up, it gives a soft sparkly look to substances, so it's often added to paint, bowling balls, make-up, and toothpaste.

China Rocks!

Over 1,400 years ago, the Chinese figured out how to make porcelain and use it in beautiful yet strong pottery. Porcelain is made from a special clay mineral called "china clay" and from feldspar. The Chinese refused to share the secret of how to make porcelain, so the Europeans had to buy porcelain from them. Porcelain cost more than gold!

CALCITE can be almost any color and can form beautiful, large crystals. Usually, though, its crystals are too small to be seen. Limestone, marble, seashells, and fossils are all made mainly from calcite.

ICE. Ice? That's a mineral? Ice is solid, it's crystalline, and it's natural. Which means that yes . . . ice is a mineral!

MINERALS INSIDE YOU!

Some plants and animals make minerals, including you! Have you ever heard that milk is good for you because it helps your bones grow? Milk contains atoms of calcium. Your body uses this calcium to make tiny crystals of the mineral apatite to form your bones and teeth. Many sea creatures make calcite to form their shells.

JUST FOR LAUGHS!

What did one tooth say to the other when it stopped chewing?

"I'VE LOST MY APATITE!"

WOW!

A crystal of beryl was found in Madagascar that is 60 feet (18 meters) long. That's longer than a school bus!

GROW LOTS OF NEEDLE-LIKE MINERAL CRYSTALS

You can grow your own crystals of the mineral epsomite.

1 First place a few Epsom salt grains on the black paper and look at them closely. What shape are the grains?

2 Now cut the paper into whatever shape you like, such as a snowflake or heart. Place the paper into the pie pan or cookie sheet. Cut the paper if it doesn't fit completely within it.

3 Slowly add the Epsom salts into the hot water, stirring constantly. Keep stirring until all of the Epsom salts are dissolved if possible. Add food coloring if you like.

4 Pour the solution over the paper. Place the cookie sheet with the paper and solution in a warm place, like a sunny window. With an adult's help, you can also place it in a 200-degree-Fahrenheit oven (93 degrees Celsius) for 15 minutes or so, but watch to make sure it doesn't dry out too much. You should start to see lots of large crystals growing.

THINGS TO NOTICE

+ What kind of "habit" do your crystals have? Cubic? Spiky?

+ Did your crystals seem to **GROW**? Where do you think they came from?

+ What do you think you could do to stop them growing? Think about what crystals need to grow.

SUPPLIES:

- 1 cup Epsom salts
- black construction paper
- magnifying glass (*optional*)
- scissors
- pie pan or cookie sheet with edges
- large measuring cup
- ½ cup hot tap water
- food coloring (*optional*)

MAKE A MODEL OF A SALT CRYSTAL

The salt that you put on your food comes from a mineral from the earth. Like all minerals, its atoms are arranged in a pattern.

1 Make a square of four gumdrops, with each gumdrop connected to the opposite color by a toothpick. The gumdrops represent the atoms and the toothpicks represent the connections between them.

2 Place your square on the table and poke a toothpick into each gumdrop so that the toothpicks point straight up. Add the opposite color gumdrop to the end of each toothpick.

3 Connect the upper layer of gumdrops with toothpicks to make a box with gumdrops in the corners. Each gumdrop should be connected to three gumdrops of the opposite color.

4 This is a simple model of a salt crystal. The red gumdrops represent sodium atoms and the green gumdrops are chlorine atoms. You can expand your salt crystal by adding more toothpicks on one side of the box, then attaching gumdrops of the opposite color.

THINGS TO NOTICE

+ This is a model of a salt crystal. To show how many atoms are in one grain of salt, it would take 100,000,000,000,000,000 more boxes like this one. There are more atoms in one grain of salt than there are people on Earth, stars in our galaxy, or grains of sand on a beach!

+ Sprinkle a few grains of salt on a dark piece of paper and look at them closely with a magnifying glass. Is the shape of the salt crystals like the shape of your salt model? Why do you think they're similar?

SUPPLIES:

○ toothpicks
○ red and green gumdrops
○ a few grains of salt
○ magnifying glass (*optional*)

WHAT MAKES A DIAMOND BLUE?

Diamonds are made of carbon atoms. Blue diamonds, like the Hope Diamond, also have some boron atoms mixed in, but not very many. As little as one boron atom in a million carbon atoms can make a diamond look blue. That's a hard number to imagine! Try this activity to get a better idea of those big numbers.

1 Measure out ½ cup of salt and place it in a bowl or on a piece of paper.

2 Place the grain of sand on top.

THINGS TO NOTICE

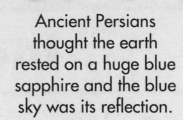

+ There are about a million grains of salt in ½ cup of salt. So the salt represents 1,000,000 atoms of carbon, and the grain of sand represents the boron atom that would make the diamond look blue. Of course a real diamond has many more atoms of both carbon and boron, and they would be in a crystal structure, not just in a pile. But the ratio would be the same. For every grain of sand (one boron atom) you add, you have to add another ½ cup of salt (one million carbon atoms).

WOW!

Ancient Persians thought the earth rested on a huge blue sapphire and the blue sky was its reflection.

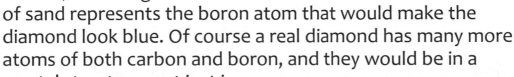

SUPPLIES:

O ½ cup salt
O measuring cup
O grain of sand or similar sized particle

IGNEOUS ROCKS

What happens when you heat chocolate? It melts, of course. When you cool the chocolate it becomes solid again. The same thing happens with rocks, except that it has to be a **LOT** hotter to melt rocks. It has to be about four times as hot as the temperature needed to bake cookies.

Where does it get that hot? Tunneling toward the center of the earth, it gets hotter and hotter. About 25 miles beneath the surface, it's hot enough to melt rocks. Molten rock beneath the surface of the earth is called magma.

Did U Know?

Igneous means fiery, or "made from fire" in Latin.

When magma forms, it slowly bubbles up to the earth's surface. The closer it gets to the surface, the cooler it becomes. So the magma cools and becomes solid—just like your chocolate! Rocks that form from cooling magma are called igneous rocks. There are two types of **IGNEOUS ROCKS**.

INTRUSIVE ROCKS

When magma cools and hardens before it reaches the surface of the earth, it forms **INTRUSIVE IGNEOUS ROCKS**. Magma can form deep underground in huge blobs many miles across. As the magma rises and cools, it forms large areas of rock. Smaller blobs of magma can break through existing solid rocks and form sheets of rock a few inches or feet thick called **DIKES**.

Igneous rocks are very hard. As softer rocks above and around them wear away, they are left standing at the surface. Long mountain chains are often intrusive igneous rocks formed from huge blobs of magma.

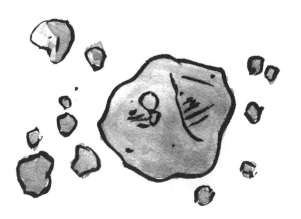

IGNEOUS ROCKS: rocks that form from cooling magma.

INTRUSIVE IGNEOUS ROCKS: rocks that form from magma cooling and becoming solid below the surface of the earth.

DIKES: a sheet of igneous rock that cuts across other rocks.

WORDS 2 KNOW

EXTRUSIVE ROCKS

Magma that rises all the way to the surface of the earth is called **LAVA**. Lava comes out through volcanoes and cools to form **EXTRUSIVE IGNEOUS ROCKS**. In most volcanoes, like the ones active in Hawaii, the lava is runny and slowly bubbles out. These volcanoes aren't dangerous.

In other volcanos, like Mt. St. Helens in the state of Washington, lava and **ASH** explode out. The volcano blows its top! Eruptions from explosive volcanoes can be dangerous. High-speed avalanches of hot ash, pieces of rock, and gas can travel up to 150 miles per hour. That's a lot faster than cars travel on the highway! **MUDFLOWS** can form that wipe out everything in their path, including boulders and houses.

WORDS 2 KNOW

LAVA: magma that comes to the surface of the earth.

EXTRUSIVE IGNEOUS ROCKS: rocks that form from lava cooling and becoming solid on the surface of the earth.

ASH: rock and glass fragments that are smaller than a pinhead, produced from an explosive volcano.

MUDFLOW: a high-speed flow of mud formed from lava and ash mixing with melted snow and rain.

Did U Know?

Some islands, like the state of Hawaii and the country of Iceland, are made up entirely of volcanic rocks.

Why are some volcanoes runny and some explosive? The runny kinds of volcanoes have lava that is thin like salad dressing. This allows gases to escape easily before the lava reaches the surface. These kinds of volcanoes are usually located where the tectonic plates are pulling apart. Many of them are under the oceans. When lava flows into oceans, it reacts with the seawater and forms rounded shapes of basalt, called pillow lava.

Explosive volcanoes have lava that is thick and pasty, like toothpaste. This causes gases to build up until they explode as the lava reaches the surface. These volcanoes are usually located around the edges of tectonic plates where one plate is pushing under another.

Try This!

Get two cans of soda. Open one can and take a few sips. Pour some of the soda into a glass and let it sit for a few hours, then taste it. Can you feel the difference in the fizz? Now go outside, shake the second can of soda, and open it. Make sure to point it away from you!.

Lava has dissolved gas in it, just like soda. Thin lava rises to the surface slowly, leaving the gas lots of time to escape. So it becomes "flat" like the first soda, and pours out onto the surface without much fizz. But when a LOT of gas stays trapped in pasty, thick lava, it acts like the soda that you've shaken. When the pressure is finally released, look out!

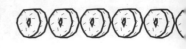

VOLCANOLOGISTS

Volcanologists are scientists who study volcanoes. They want to understand volcanoes because they are curious. They also want to be able to predict what volcanoes will do, so they can warn people living near volcanoes before eruptions. Their dangerous job includes taking samples of volcanic gases and lava. Here are some things that volcanologists do to protect themselves:

Do you have a buddy on field trips? Volcanologists have a buddy when they get close to volcanoes and they watch out for each other.

Lava is HOT—about 1,800 degrees Fahrenheit (982 degrees Celsius). This is WAY hotter than your oven. Volcanologists wear suits made out of a special fabric that reflects the heat and doesn't catch fire.

Lava is bright—so bright it can blind people! Volcanologists wear a helmet and hood with special glasses to protect their eyes from the super-bright lava.

The air around active volcanoes can contain toxic gases. Volcanologists wear breathing masks to protect them from harmful gases.

Not all of the work that volcanologists do is right next to volcanoes. They also collect lots of other information. Sometimes earthquakes occur shortly before volcanoes erupt, so volcanologists keep a close watch on earthquakes.

Solid Rock!

Most buildings are built from many materials. But there are 11 churches in Lalibela, Ethiopia, in Africa that weren't "built" at all. They were carved out of solid volcanic rock! The roofs of the churches are even with the ground, with a deep trench surrounding them. To enter the churches, you have to go down many steps to the bottom of the trench.

Almost 1,000 years ago, King Gadla Lalibela was inspired in a dream to build these churches. They were carved from tuff, a soft rock made of tightly packed volcanic ash. Underneath the tuff, at the base of the churches, there is basalt, another volcanic rock that is harder. The volcanic rocks probably formed about 30 million years ago.

On November 14, 1963, fishermen in the Atlantic Ocean south of Iceland noticed smoke rising from the water. By the next morning, Surtsey Island had appeared! After four days, it was 197 feet (60 kilometers) high. Where did it come from? Brand new volcanic rocks! Surtsey Island, like Iceland, formed when plates in the earth's crust pulled apart and magma from deep within the earth bubbled up.

WORDS 2 KNOW

BLACK SMOKERS: a sea vent that spews black smoke and very hot, mineral-rich water.

COARSE-GRAINED: rocks that have mineral grains that are large enough to see with just your eyes.

FINE-GRAINED: rocks that have mineral grains that are too small to see with just your eyes.

Black Smokers! Giant Tube Worms!

Far down in the ocean, where no sunlight reaches, scientists have discovered openings in the earth's crust that shoot out very hot water. This water comes from deep within the earth. It has minerals that contain sulfur, which make the water look black. The sulfur containing minerals from rocks shaped like chimneys up to 33 feet (10 meters) tall. The openings and rocks are called **BLACK SMOKERS.**

Sulfur, which smells like rotten eggs, is poisonous to most animals. But there's a type of bacteria that loves it, and uses sulfur to make its own food. These bacteria live inside the bodies of other ocean creatures, including giant tube worms that can grow longer than 10 feet (3 meters). The worms don't have a mouth or a stomach, and they don't eat—they just survive off the bacteria.

More than 50 volcanoes in the United States have erupted in the past 200 years, mostly in Hawaii, Alaska, California, Oregon, and Washington.

Did U Know?

BIG GRAINS, LITTLE GRAINS, NO GRAINS

When magma cools, the atoms arrange themselves into patterns that form crystals. When the magma cools slowly, like it does for intrusive rocks, the atoms have lots of time to arrange themselves. They build lots of layers that form large crystals. Rocks with large crystals are called **COARSE-GRAINED**. Intrusive rocks can take thousands, even millions, of years to cool because the surrounding rocks are warm.

When the magma cools quickly, like it does when a volcano erupts and releases lava, the atoms don't have much time to arrange themselves. The crystals that form are too small to see without a microscope. Rocks like these take only weeks or days to form and are called **FINE-GRAINED**. Sometimes, the lava cools so fast that it can't form crystals at all. When this happens the magma produces volcanic glass.

WOW!

In 1815, the Tambora volcano in Indonesia suffered the most powerful eruption in recorded history.
It released so much ash and gases that it blocked out some sunlight and caused the entire earth to become cooler. The next year was called "The Year without a Summer," because it snowed year-round in Europe and North America. Imagine snow in July!

 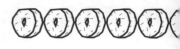
COMMON IGNEOUS ROCKS

GRANITE is one of the best-known types of rock. Many buildings, kitchen countertops, and statues are made of granite. It is white, gray, or pale pink in color and coarse-grained. You can easily see the individual minerals. Granite is made of quartz, feldspar, and mica. It can look sparkly in the sunlight because tiny bits of mica reflect the light. The minerals that form granite aren't as dense as others, so even though granite feels heavy to us, it's lighter than other igneous rocks.

Granite is an intrusive rock. It forms when magma rising towards the surface of the earth doesn't quite reach the surface, and slowly cools.

PEGMATITES, like granite, are also intrusive rocks. They are formed from the very last part of magma to cool. This magma has more water in it, which allows very large crystals to form. Some crystals are as big as logs!

Like granite, pegmatites usually contain quartz, feldspar, and mica. They can also hold rare minerals, such as topaz and sapphires.

Wow! Pow! Look out Below!

About 2.1 million years ago, a volcanic eruption in Yellowstone National Park, Wyoming, spewed out so much ash that it could have covered the entire western half of the United States in 4 feet of it!

Did U Know?

BASALT is an extrusive rock that is dark brownish-gray and very fine-grained. You can't see the individual minerals without a microscope. Basalt is made of feldspar, pyroxene, and a small amount of quartz. These dense minerals make basalt heavy and give it its dark color. Basalt forms when magma rises to the surface and erupts as lava from volcanoes.

When the lava contains lots of gas bubbles, they become trapped as it cools. This produces basalt with a rough texture. Sometimes you can see the little holes where the gas was trapped. Basalt can even form in columns with six sides, probably formed from cracks as the lava was cooling.

OBSIDIAN has sharp edges and a surface that looks like glass. That's because it is glass! Sometimes, lava exploding from volcanoes cools so quickly that the atoms don't have time to arrange themselves into patterns before forming solid rock. As a result, they make a type of glass—not too different from the glass in a bottle or window. But you can't see through obsidian because it contains chemicals that give it a dark color.

Ancient people used obsidian to make weapons. Even now, people use obsidian to make scalpel blades for surgery because it has very thin, sharp edges.

JUST FOR LAUGHS!

What did one igneous rock say to another at dinner?

PLEASE PASS THE BASALT!

Basalt covers more of the earth's surface than any other rock, because it forms almost all of the oceanic crust. If you dug under the thin layer of sediment at the bottom of the oceans, you'd find basalt.

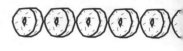

Devils Tower in Wyoming and the Giant's Causeway in Ireland are two famous examples of basalt cooling into columns.

Did U Know?

PUMICE is another kind of glassy rock. It is usually white, with lots of holes. When magma deep within the earth rises very quickly, gases trapped in the magma bubble out.

When there are lots of gases and the magma rises especially fast, it can be a frothy mixture of gases and liquid rock. Pumice comes from this frothy mixture. The holes in pumice were left by all of the gas bubbles, and the solid parts are glass because the lava cooled so fast. Pumice is used in pencil erasers and to make stonewashed jeans.

Pumice is the only rock that floats on water!

Pumice Rafts

Pumice that lands in the ocean can form rafts that float for a long time. These rafts can transport coral colonies, barnacles, marine worms, and algae from one place to another before they finally sink. When a volcanic island in Indonesia, named Krakatoa exploded, rafts of pumice drifted on the Pacific Ocean for 20 years!

Make Your Own Basalt Columns

Scientists use cornstarch and water to study how basalt cools and forms columns. You can try the same thing. The only difference between what you and scientists do is that they have powerful microscopes to examine what is happening at a microscopic level.

1 Mix equal parts of cornstarch and water in the pie pan until the pan is about half full. Stir well.

2 Set the pie pan under a bright light for one week, or until it is completely dry. The light should be several inches above the pan. You can also use a sunny windowsill. First you'll see cracks that break the cornstarch into shapes. Keep it under the light until you see much finer cracks at the top. The longer it dries, the better.

3 Hold up the pie pan and look at the bottom. Do you see any shapes? Carefully pry up pieces of cornstarch and look to see if it formed columns. Do they have a particular shape? If you don't see columns allow the cornstarch to dry out more.

Things to Notice

+ Most liquids shrink when they cool and become solid. Lava does too. Do you think that has anything to do with the columns in basalt and your cornstarch? Have you ever seen mud when it dries? Does it have cracks?

Supplies:

- O transparent pie pan
- O measuring cup
- O 1 cup cornstarch
- O 1 cup warm tap water
- O spoon
- O bright light

Make Meringue

CAUTION: This project involves using the oven, so get an adult to help.

Have you ever eaten a rock? These cookies aren't exactly rocks, but they look like them. Make these cookies on a cool, dry day. In hot, humid weather, the meringue doesn't dry properly.

1 Preheat the oven to 250 degrees Fahrenheit (121 degrees Celsius) and put the oven rack in the center position. Line a cookie sheet with wax paper.

2 Hold an egg lightly with one hand, and with the other hand, crack the eggshell firmly with the butter knife.

SUPPLIES:

- O oven
- O cookie sheet
- O wax paper
- O 6 eggs at room temperature
- O butter knife
- O two small bowls
- O large metal or glass bowl
- O ¼ teaspoon cream of tartar or white vinegar
- O electric mixer
- O ½ cup sugar
- O ¼ teaspoon vanilla (optional)

3 Pull the eggshell apart without letting the yolk fall into the bowl. Pour the yolk back and forth between the eggshell halves, letting the egg white fall into the bowl. Keep the yolk in the shell and be careful that it doesn't break. When all of the white is in the bowl, put the yolk into the other bowl to use for another cooking project, or throw it away.

"Pumice" Cookies

4 Pour the white from the small bowl into the large bowl, so that if you break a yolk on the next egg, you won't ruin the whole batch. Repeat this process for the rest of the eggs.

5 Add the cream of tartar or vinegar to the egg whites in the large bowl. Beat the mixture with an electric mixer on high until the egg whites get foamy and form soft peaks that gently flop over when you remove the beaters.

6 Gradually add the sugar and vanilla and keep beating just until the meringue is shiny, smooth, and stands up in a peak about 2 inches high.

7 Drop big blobs of the meringue onto the wax paper on the cookie sheet and bake for 1 hour 30 minutes. The meringue should look dry, stiff, and very light brown. Turn off the oven and let the meringue cookies cool completely in the oven before you take them out—at least one hour.

8 Clean up carefully! You don't get to lick the bowl in this recipe because raw eggs can make you sick. For the same reason, make sure you use paper towels to wipe up any spilled raw egg, then throw them in the trash.

Things to Notice

+ Is your "pumice" lighter than other cookies the same size? Why do you think that is? Break one in half and look at the broken edge. What do you see? Does this have anything to do with how light your cookie is? Why do you think pumice is the only rock that can float on water?

41

MAKE YOUR OWN
IGNEOUS ROCKS

CAUTION: This project involves very hot liquids, so get an adult to help.

When a volcano erupts, the rocks that form can have minerals that are big enough to see, or so small they can't be seen. Sometimes a mineral doesn't form at all and the rock is a glass. Try some of your own "lava" to see why each of these types of rocks form.

1 Grease the cookie sheet with cooking spray and place it in the freezer.

2 Tie one end of the string to a button and wrap the other end around a pencil. Place the pencil on top of one of the glass jars so that the string hangs down into the jar. Adjust the length of the string so that the button is just above the bottom of the glass. Do the same thing with the second jar.

3 Pour about 1½ cups of water into a saucepan and add about 3 cups of sugar. Heat the sugar-water mixture until it boils, stirring until the sugar dissolves or the syrup has small bubbles in it. **Have an adult help you with this part.**

4 Cook the sugar syrup over medium heat for 3 minutes without stirring. Remove the saucepan from the heat and let cool for 2 minutes.

5 With your adult helper, carefully pour the syrup into each jar to just below the brim. If there is extra sugar on the bottom of the saucepan, do not let it flow into the jars. Using a potholder, move the jars to a warm place where they can be easily seen, but will not be disturbed.

6 Put the remaining cup of sugar in the saucepan. Heat the sugar on low to medium until the sugar turns brown and melts. Be patient—it will take about 10 minutes. As soon as the sugar melts completely, get an adult to help you pour it into the cookie sheet. Be very careful—the sugar is very hot.

7 Place the cookie sheet in the refrigerator or freezer until the sugar syrup has hardened, about 10 minutes. Then pry the sugar glass out of the cookie sheet and look at it carefully. Do you see any crystals?

8 Set aside your sugar glass while you wait for crystals to grow on the cotton string. Be patient! After a few days, take out one of the strings with small sugar crystals. Wait for at least a week before taking the second string out. The longer you wait, the bigger the sugar crystal will grow. If no crystal forms, or if the whole glass of syrup turns into a solid lump, you may have stirred it while it was boiling. Try again!

THINGS TO NOTICE

+ Compare your three examples of sugar. How do you think they might compare to hot magma or lava cooling?

+ Which type of your crystals do you think might represent magma that cools underground and has a lot of time to cool?

+ Which type do you think might represent lava that cools quickly on the surface?

+ Which type do you think cools so quickly that crystals can't form?

SUPPLIES:

- 0 cookie sheet with sides
- 0 freezer
- 0 cooking spray
- 0 cotton string
- 0 two buttons
- 0 two pencils
- 0 two glass jars
- 0 water
- 0 saucepan
- 0 4 cups sugar
- 0 potholder
- 0 stove

43

SEDIMENTARY ROCKS

Everyone loves the beach. The crashing waves and the flowing sand make for great fun. Sand is also central to the second major rock type: SEDIMENTARY ROCKS. These are rocks made from SEDIMENTS, or tiny particles that are pressed tightly together into stone.

Standing on a beach, you're looking at the ingredients for future sedimentary rocks. To understand how most sedimentary rocks are formed, you must understand how the sand got to the beach in the first place. It happens through a process called **EROSION**.

EROSION

Imagine that you're a huge boulder high on a mountain. For the first few thousand years or so, you think you're indestructible. But slowly, rain and wind and ice work on you.

One winter, you crack a little bit. Water drips into these cracks and freezes, and the crack gets bigger. Maybe wind knocks a rock against you, breaking off a piece. Before you know it—after many more thousands of years, that is—you're nothing more than a load of smaller rocks tumbling down the mountainside.

During a rainstorm, you're swept into a stream. In the stream you're broken down into smaller rocks, and your sharp edges are smoothed. These small pieces of rock are called sediments, like pebbles, sand, and mud. You might settle at the bottom of a river, or be carried out to the ocean, or be blown by the air to become part of a sand dune. But one thing is for sure: you've been eroded!

SEDIMENTARY ROCKS: rocks formed from sediments, the remains of plants or animals, or from the evaporation of seawater.

SEDIMENTS: small particles of rocks or minerals, such as clay, sand, or pebbles.

EROSION: the process where rocks are broken down by wind, water, ice, and gravity, and then carried away.

 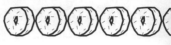

CLASTIC SEDIMENTARY ROCKS

The most common sedimentary rocks on Earth are **CLASTIC SEDIMENTARY ROCKS**. These are rocks formed from sediments—also called **CLASTS**—pressed together into rock.

First, water **DEPOSITS** layers of sediments, one on top of another. As the top layers add up, they bury the lower layers and press them together. As the lower layers are buried farther and farther below the surface, they also heat up. The heat and pressure change the soft sediments—like that beach sand—into hard rocks.

Usually, water that contains minerals dissolved in it soaks the sediments. As the clasts become hotter, the water dries and the minerals left behind "glue" the sediments together.

Clastic rocks are divided into groups based on the size of the sediments in them. Usually, clastic rocks formed from large sediments, like pebbles, haven't traveled very far from their **PARENT ROCK**. Rocks with very small clasts, like clay particles, usually have traveled many, many miles from their parent rock. This makes sense because large, heavy sediments can't move very far in water or air before dropping out due to their weight. Tiny particles can be blown or carried quite far.

WORDS 2 KNOW

CLASTIC SEDIMENTARY ROCKS: sedimentary rocks that form from rock fragments, or clasts, pressed together.

CLASTS: rock fragments such as pebbles, sand, or clay.

DEPOSIT: leave behind. For example, muddy water can deposit mud as it flows over a surface or evaporates.

PARENT ROCK: the original rock from which another rock was formed.

BEDS: layers of sedimentary rocks.

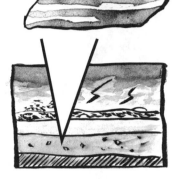

Sediments usually build up layer by layer. When those sediments turn into rocks, the rocks display these layers. There can even be **BEDS**, or layers, of different kinds of rock, one on top of the other. Originally, layers of sediments are horizontal, because gravity pulls on the sediments. But once they become rocks, the layers can be tilted by forces in the earth.

CONGLOMERATES are clastic sedimentary rocks that consist of large pebbles stuck together by sand and other materials. One type of conglomerate is called the puddingstone, because the pebbles look like raisins in a pudding. Yum!

First Things First

In the 1600s, people thought that rocks didn't change very much at all after they were created. A man named Nicolas Steno disagreed. Steno suggested that layers of rock were deposited one on top of another, with the oldest beds at the bottom and the youngest at the top. Steno also said that sedimentary layers were first laid down in flat, horizontal beds, and then folded or tilted later.

This may seem like common sense to us now, but at the time, it was a revolutionary idea. It suggested that rocks tell a story. For this reason, Steno has been called "the founder of geology."

SANDSTONE is a clastic sedimentary rock usually made of the mineral quartz. The grains that make up the rock are the size of sand that you find on the beach. These grains have been pressed together with mineral "glue." Like sand, sandstone can be any color, but is most commonly yellow, red, tan, brown, or white.

WORDS 2 KNOW

ORGANIC SEDIMENTARY ROCKS: sedimentary rocks that form from the remains of plants or animals.

Other kinds of rocks formed from grains compressed together are shale, mudstone, and claystone. These are made from smaller grains. The grains in claystone are so small that you can't see them with just your eyes.

ORGANIC SEDIMENTARY ROCKS

Life on Earth depends on minerals and rocks in many ways. But living things also help to make new rocks, including sedimentary rocks. Many sedimentary rocks are formed from the remains of plants and animals. These are called **ORGANIC SEDIMENTARY ROCKS**, because organic means living.

Uluru is a huge chunk of sandstone in central Australia. Also called Ayers Rock, it is the world's largest single block of freestanding rock. Uluru rises 1,142 feet (863 meters) above the ground, but it extends deep into the earth. The layers of rock were originally horizontal, like all sedimentary rocks. But they were tilted by movement in the earth, so now they're almost vertical!

Did U Know?

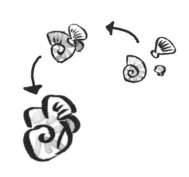

Sea creatures leave behind shells made of calcite that are glued together to form limestone. The remains of plants and animals form coal, oil, and natural gas, which we use to fuel our cars and heat our homes. The shells that you see at the beach or the plants growing in a nearby swamp may some day be part of rocks!

LIMESTONE is a pale tan or gray organic sedimentary rock made mostly of the mineral calcite. It comes from sea creatures like corals and mollusks. These animals absorb mineral particles from the water around them to form their shells. After the animals die, their shells fall to the ocean floor, where they are pressed together into limestone.

COAL is a black or dark brown rock that burns. People have burned it for thousands of years to produce heat. Today, we use coal to generate electricity. Believe it or not, coal is formed from the remains of living things.

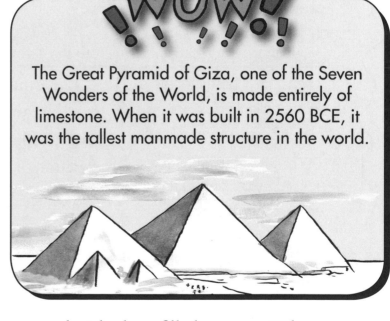

The Great Pyramid of Giza, one of the Seven Wonders of the World, is made entirely of limestone. When it was built in 2560 BCE, it was the tallest manmade structure in the world.

Before dinosaurs lived— 300 million years ago—the earth was covered with plant-filled swamps. When the plants died, they sank into the swamps and were covered with sand and mud. As time went on, more and more sediments buried the plant remains. Eventually, they turned into coal. Just think, without sedimentary rocks like coal, we wouldn't have the energy to power our homes!

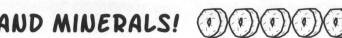

CHEMICAL SEDIMENTARY ROCKS

Sedimentary rocks are also formed from **SOLUTIONS**. A solution consists of water with a mineral—like salt—dissolved in it. When the water **EVAPORATES**, the mineral is left behind. This is called an **EVAPORITE**. If enough of the evaporite mineral builds up, a **CHEMICAL SEDIMENTARY ROCK** forms. Evaporites usually form when shallow inland seas slowly dry up, leaving minerals behind.

Do you live where it snows? If you get a big snowstorm, you get to stay home. But if you only get a little snow, you still probably have to go to school. The mineral halite, called rock salt, is likely the reason why. When snow is mixed with salt, it melts, because salt water freezes at a lower temperature than freshwater. During snowstorms, trucks sprinkle salt on roads to melt the snow and make the roads less slippery. So you can go to school!

LIMESTONE can also form as a chemical sedimentary rock. Seawater contains dissolved calcite, so limestone can form when seawater evaporates. When limestone dissolves, the erosion creates caves and their many beautiful formations.

Limestone is used in cement and toothpaste. It can even be ground up and put in bread and cereal as a source of calcium.

ROCK SALT is the mineral halite, a clear or white mineral found in evaporite deposits. Seawater contains a lot of salt. If you collected a 2-liter bottle of seawater, it would contain about 5 tablespoons of salt. When shallow seas evaporate, they leave deposits of salt behind. In the Dead Sea in the country of Jordan, the water is so salty that it leaves deposits of salt on its shores and bottom.

Salty Hotel

The Salt Palace and Spa in Bolivia is the world's only hotel made of salt. The walls are made of 14-inch blocks of salt cemented together with salt water. The roof, floors, and

furniture are also made of salt! Built in 1993, the hotel sits in the middle of the Uyuni Salt Flats.

Salt flats are exactly that: huge flat zones of salt. Long ago, these salt flats were salt water lakes. As the lake evaporated over time, the salt was left behind. Today, the salt is mined for table salt.

Salt is used to make certain chemicals, like baking soda, and of course, we use salt to season our food.

GYPSUM is also dissolved in seawater. When seawater evaporates from shallow inland seas, it leaves this soft, white or transparent mineral behind. Gypsum can be found all over the world, often in thick beds. Very fine-grained gypsum is called alabaster, and is used to make beautiful sculptures. People have mined gypsum since ancient times to make mortar and plaster. Today, gypsum is also used for walls inside houses.

WORDS 2 KNOW

SOLUTION: a fluid with a substance dissolved in it. Salt water is a solution.

EVAPORATE: when a liquid turns into a gas.

EVAPORITE: a mineral that forms by the evaporation of seawater, leaving dissolved minerals behind. Examples are salt and gypsum.

CHEMICAL SEDIMENTARY ROCK: sedimentary rock that forms when water that contains dissolved minerals evaporates and leaves behind the mineral deposits.

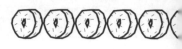
CAVES!

Caves are holes beneath the surface of the earth that are usually formed from limestone. Rainwater sometimes contains dissolved gases that make it **ACIDIC**. Liquids that are acidic can dissolve other materials. When rainwater trickles down to limestone beneath the surface of the earth, it dissolves the limestone, creating caves.

Sometimes caves contain fascinating **STALACTITES** and **STALAGMITES**. Stalactites are formations that hang down from the ceilings of caves (the word stalactites has a "c" for ceiling) and stalagmites rise from the ground (think "g" for ground). How do they form? As rainwater seeps through limestone and dissolves it, the minerals forming the limestone dissolve in the water. As the water drips down, it leaves behind traces of limestone. Drop by drop, huge stalactites and stalagmites form.

WORDS 2 KNOW

ACIDIC: acids are chemicals that taste sour. Examples are vinegar, lemon juice, and acids in your stomach.

STALACTITE: a cave formation that looks like an icicle hanging from the ceiling.

STALAGMITE: a cave formation projecting up from the floor, often underneath a stalactite.

HAVE A SED-SANDWICH FOR LUNCH

1 Spread mustard or mayonnaise on one piece of bread with the table knife. Place lettuce on top.

2 Add whatever cold cuts you like on top of the lettuce, then another piece of bread.

3 Add more mustard or mayonnaise to the top of the bread. Add more cold cuts, then the last piece of bread. Cut your sed-sandwich in half and enjoy!

THINGS TO NOTICE

+ How is your sed-sandwich like a sedimentary rock? Which layers of your sandwich were "deposited" first? Which last? Do you think rocks form in the same way?

+ Most important question of all: which do you think tastes better, your sed-sandwich or sandstone?

SUPPLIES:

O 3 pieces of bread
O mustard or mayonnaise
O table knife
O lettuce
O cold cuts such as sliced cheese, ham, turkey, etc.

Did U Know?

Caves can be enormous!

The cave in Mammoth Cave National Park is at least 365 miles long (they haven't finished exploring it!). If you walked one mile every single day for a year, you would just get to the end of parts of the cave that have already been explored.

Make Your Own Stalactites

1 Fill the cups about half full with hot water. Stir in Epsom salts until no more will dissolve.

2 Cut about 18 inches (46 centimeters) of string. Tie two paper clips to each end and place the entire string in one cup.

3 Place the cups about 1 foot apart with the dish between, in a place where they won't be disturbed.

4 Pull the string out and drape the string between the cups. The paper clips should rest in the bottom of each cup.

There should be a slight droop to the string, but don't let it touch the dish. Check the project each day. Do you have any stalactites or stalagmites?

Things to Notice

+ Where do you think the Epsom salts went when you put them in the hot water? How did your stalactites and stalagmites get there? What do you think they're made of?

Supplies:

0 2 glasses or cups
0 hot tap water
0 Epsom salts
0 cotton or wool string
0 4 paper clips
0 dish

Make Your Own Sedimentary Rock

1 With an adult's help, cut off the top of the soda bottle using the scissors.

2 Mix about ½ cup sand with ½ cup plaster of Paris in the bowl. Pour the mixture into the empty soda bottle.

3 Repeat step 2 with other sediments such as gravel and pebbles. Mix the same amount of plaster of Paris and sediment together before pouring into the soda bottle. You can also add a layer of just plaster of Paris. If you like, push seashells into one or more layers.

4 Slowly pour water into the soda bottle until it just covers the top layer. Wait one or more days until everything is dry. Cut away the soda bottle. You now have a sedimentary rock!

!WOW!

White Sands National Monument in New Mexico has the largest gypsum sand dunes in the world—as high as 60 feet (18 meters). The sand there is bright white, powdery, and soft. Visitors often go sledding down the sides of the dunes!

SUPPLIES:

- scissors
- empty 2-liter soda bottle, label removed
- large bowl and spoon
- measuring cup
- sand
- plaster of Paris, from a hardware or craft store
- small pieces of gravel (smaller than a penny)
- pebbles of various sizes
- one or more seashells *(optional)*
- water

MAKE YOUR OWN EVAPORITE

1 Fill the bowl about two-thirds full with hot tap water. Scoop small spoonfuls of salt into the water.

2 Stir the mixture with the large spoon after each spoonful is added. Keep adding salt until it doesn't dissolve anymore.

3 Pour the mixture into the baking pan. Set the pan in a place where it won't be disturbed, ideally in a warm windowsill.

4 Check the pan after a day. Is there still water? Do you see any crystals forming? Keep checking until all of the water has evaporated.

THINGS TO NOTICE

+ Do you think the salt disappeared when you mixed it in the water? Where do you think it went? Where do you think the water went after a few days? What do you think would happen if you added hot water to your salt crystals again? Try it and see if you're right.

SUPPLIES:

- ○ small mixing bowl
- ○ hot tap water
- ○ table salt
- ○ large and small spoon
- ○ shallow baking pan

METAMORPHIC ROCKS

Have you ever seen a caterpillar change into a butterfly? It's an amazing change—if you didn't see it, you might not believe that such a delicate creature could come from a fat caterpillar. The caterpillar METAMORPHOSED, or completely changed its nature and appearance. That's what the third kind of rocks, metamorphic rocks, are all about: change. METAMORPHIC ROCKS form when heat or pressure changes existing rocks into new rocks.

Metamorphic rocks are often very hard and dense rocks. The pressures that create them pack their atoms even more closely together. Many of the oldest rocks in the world are metamorphic rocks because they are located where they couldn't erode.

HEAT + PRESSURE = ROCK MAKEOVER!

When heat or pressure is applied to rocks, they change. A LOT of heat and pressure, like that in the mantle deep under the earth's surface, melts rocks into magma. A LITTLE heat and pressure, like that close to the surface, glues grains together into sedimentary rocks.

Between these extremes, rocks exposed to heat or pressure change, as the atoms in the minerals slowly rearrange themselves into new crystals. They remain solid during the process. If you mold something out of clay and leave it in a warm place, it may slowly sink down. If you put pressure on the clay by pushing down with your hand, you can change its shape more. Similar things happen with rocks, except at much higher temperatures and pressures. Atoms pack closer together because of increased pressures, causing **RECRYSTALLIZATION.**

WORDS 2 KNOW

METAMORPHOSE: to completely change something's nature or appearance.

METAMORPHIC ROCKS: rocks that have been transformed by heat or pressure or both into new rocks, while staying solid.

RECRYSTALLIZATION: during metamorphism, when atoms in the minerals pack closer together to form new crystals because of greater pressures and heat.

CONTACT METAMORPHISM: metamorphism that happens when rocks come into contact with hot magma.

In rocks that contain lots of different kinds of atoms, new minerals may form as the atoms rearrange themselves. In other cases, the minerals may stay the same, but their crystals may get larger or smaller. The metamorphic rocks that form depend on the heat or pressure applied and the original kinds of rocks.

The oldest rock is a gneiss rock in northern Canada. It's over four billion years old!

What happens if you squish down clay, then take your hand off? It doesn't spring back up—it stays squished. Metamorphic rocks are the same way. The new minerals and the new crystal structures "lock in" at the higher temperatures and pressures and usually stay that way, even as the rocks cool.

CONTACT METAMORPHISM

Sometimes, when blobs of very hot magma from deep within the mantle rise up through the earth's crust, they cook the surrounding rocks.

In this type of metamorphism, called **CONTACT METAMORPHISM**, the igneous rocks formed from the cooled magma have a ring of metamorphosed rocks around them. The ring can be just an inch or two wide, or miles across. How much a rock is affected depends on its distance from magma, and how big and hot the blob of magma is. Rocks close to the magma heat up and change more than rocks far away from the magma.

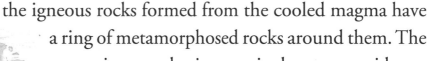

REGIONAL METAMORPHISM

When one section of crust crashes into another, the crust piles up on top of itself and forms long mountain chains at the plate boundaries. As the rocks pile up, temperatures and pressures at the center increase. The rocks there are cooked and crushed! This pressure cooking produces **REGIONAL METAMORPHISM**, because the changes happen over large regions.

Layers

Layering in rocks is common. In sedimentary rocks, layering forms where different types of rocks form on top of each other or from rocks having different sized grains. During metamorphism, new crystals are forming under a lot of pressure. Many of the minerals, like mica and chlorite, form flat crystals, which grow outward at right angles from the force of pressure. Layering is called bedding in sedimentary rocks and called **FOLIATION** in metamorphic rocks.

High Grade or Low Grade?

Do rocks get a grade like an A or an F? No, the "grade" of metamorphism is the amount of metamorphism, or heat and pressure that the rock has been under. Rocks that experience greater pressure and higher temperatures will change more. These rocks are called high-grade metamorphic rocks. Rocks that experience lower temperatures and pressure are called low-grade metamorphic rocks.

Why do we care what grade of metamorphism a rock has experienced? Because it tells us a lot about where that rock once was. For example, there are some minerals that only form at certain depths beneath the surface. Geologists can understand some of the history of an area from the kinds of metamorphic rocks there. It's like putting together a puzzle.

At the same time they're being formed, these regional metamorphic rocks are also being pushed and shoved by the rocks around them. Because they're hot, they're soft and often fold.

With all of this happening deep beneath the surface, how do we see these rocks? Over time, as the rocks cool, they are pushed up towards the surface. The rocks above them slowly erode away. So if you see a large area of metamorphic rocks, you'll know that there used to be many rocks above them.

WORDS 2 KNOW

REGIONAL METAMORPHISM: metamorphism that happens over large regions, usually forming long mountain chains.

FOLIATION: flat layers within metamorphic rocks. The layers form as minerals grow under pressure.

EARTH: THE ORIGINAL RECYCLER

The earth has been recycling materials for over four billion years! Every rock that you see has come from another kind of rock. And every rock that you see will eventually become another one.

Igneous rocks can be eroded into sediments. Sediments become sedimentary rocks. Those sedimentary rocks can then be buried and heated and squeezed to form metamorphic rocks. Metamorphic rocks can be pushed down into the mantle and melted, to later form igneous rocks.

If you're wondering why you don't see these

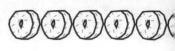

Any kind of rock, including igneous, metamorphic, and even other sedimentary rocks, can be broken down into sediments to form sedimentary rocks. Likewise, any kind of rock can change into a metamorphic rock or igneous rock.

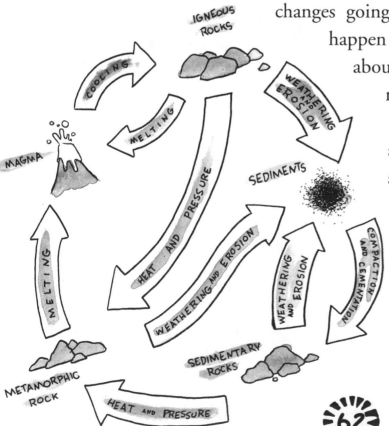

changes going on, it's because they usually happen very slowly. On average, only about one half of a millimeter of rock erodes from land surfaces each year. That's about as big as the period at the end of this sentence. Over millions of years, though, erosion can take down the highest mountains.

The time for rock material to cycle through the mantle and rise up to the crust again as magma takes hundreds of millions of years.

COMMON METAMORPHIC ROCKS

QUARTZITE is white or gray, with a **TEXTURE** like sugar. It is usually non-foliated, which means it doesn't have layers. Its parent rock is quartz sandstone, a sedimentary rock. Quartzite forms when quartz sandstone is placed under pressure and heats up, so the "glue" holding the quartz grains together disappears. This causes the grains to recrystallize. The crystals become larger and interlock. Quartzite can form under many different temperatures and pressures.

Quartzite is very hard. It often forms cliffs because it doesn't erode easily. People use quartzite for floors and stairs in buildings because it's so hard.

WORDS 2 KNOW

TEXTURE: the size, shape, and arrangement of grains or crystals in a rock.

Rocks Have Parents Too

All metamorphic rocks started out as other rocks. They may have been igneous rocks, sedimentary rocks, or even other metamorphic rocks. The starting rocks are called parent rocks. You can often tell what the parent rock was for a metamorphic rock, or at least narrow down the possibilities. It's like guessing what ingredients were used to make a cake. In an apple cake you may not know exactly how much flour was used, or if it contains milk. But you know that apples were one of the ingredients. It's the same way with rocks.

Michelangelo Carved Metamorphic Rock

One of the finest sculptures in the world is a statue of David, from the story of David and Goliath. It was sculpted by Michelangelo in 1504 out of marble and stands about 17 feet (5 meters) tall.

MARBLE is used by artists more than any other rock for carving sculptures. Marble is beautiful, and usually white or ivory colored, although it also comes in different colors. Often, these colors show up in swirling patterns. Marble's parent rock is limestone, a sedimentary rock composed of the mineral calcite. Like quartzite, marble is usually non-foliated. When marble forms, the grains of calcite in limestone recrystallize into larger, interlocking crystals.

Marble is valued for carving because it's relatively soft and doesn't shatter. It also glows when it's polished, so sculptures look life-like.

ROCKS FROM SHALE OR MUDSTONE

When the parent rock is shale, mudstone, or claystone, the kind of metamorphic rock that forms depends on how much heat or pressure there is. These rocks usually form from regional metamorphism in large belts. The highest grade rocks—gneiss—are at the core, surrounded by schist, and then slate towards the outer areas.

SLATE is a result of low-grade metamorphism of shale and mudstone. Slate is dark gray, sometimes with a blue or green tint. It can also be red or brown.

JUST FOR LAUGHS!

What did the slate say to the gneiss when report cards came out?

UGH! YOU GOT A HIGHER GRADE THAN ME!

The Taj Mahal in Agra, India, was constructed of huge blocks of marble. The blocks were transported by special carts pulled by teams of up to 30 oxen.

The grains in slate are too small to see well. When shale becomes buried and heats up, the clay minerals in shale change to mica minerals and chlorite. These minerals tend to arrange themselves in one direction, which is why slate splits into smooth, flat sheets. Slate forms under relatively low temperatures and pressures.

Slate has been used for roofs for thousands of years because it stands up well to rain and wind and is easily broken into flat sheets.

SCHIST is a result of medium-grade metamorphism. It is usually silvery gray, brown, or yellow, and it looks shiny because it has lots of mica in it. The mica also gives it strong foliation, or layering. The grains in schist are large enough to see without a magnifying glass. Schist has the same parent rock as slate, but schist rocks form deeper underground where there are higher temperatures and pressures.

Schist isn't usually used as a building material because it isn't as strong as some other metamorphic rocks. The mica in it makes schist flake off easily.

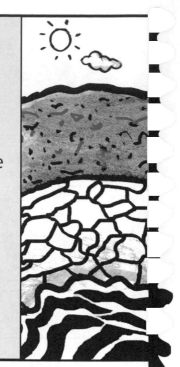

What Rock is Where?

❄ **Surface Sediment:**
Clay or Mud | Sand | Marine Animal Shells

❄ **3 miles (5 kilometers) Deep, Sedimentary Rock:**
Shale or Mudstone | Quartz or Sandstone | Limestone

❄ **6 miles (10 kilometers) Deep, Metamorphic Rock:**
Slate | Quartzite | Marble

❄ **9 miles (15 kilometers) Deep, Metamorphic Rock:**
Schist | Quartzite | Marble

❄ **12 miles (20 kilometers) Deep, Metamorphic Rock:**
Gneiss | Quartzite | Marble

GNEISS is a result of high-grade metamorphism. Pronounced "nice," gneiss usually has stripes of dark gray and light-colored minerals. Gneiss rocks tend to form deep underground, forming the core of long mountain chains. Because it's so tough, many gneiss rocks are very old. Gneiss can have shale or mudstone or granite as its parent rock. These rocks are beautiful and hard, so they are often used for counter tops and flooring.

FULGURITE has a strange name that means "thunderbolt" in Latin. It has an even stranger way of forming. When lightning hits sand, fulgurite is born! The extremely high temperature of the thunderbolt melts the sand grains together into glass tubes. Fulgurites are definitely formed from contact metamorphism!

Make Your Own FOLDED ROCKS

1 Roll out each color of clay as big and thick as a pancake. Stack the layers of clay. These are like layers of rocks.

2 With the layers flat on the table, push from both sides. If the clay sticks to the table, lift the middle up into a fold. Your hands are like forces pushing when two continents collide. The middle is a fold.

3 Saw through one end of the folded layers with the knife. If a road were cut through the rocks, this is what you might see.

4 Slice off the top at a slight angle. This is what happens when rocks are worn away, or eroded, by wind and rain.

5 Try it again, pushing the fold over on its side. Try cutting through the layers at different angles. Each time it will look a little different—just like real rocks!

6 After you make one set of folds, try pushing from the other ends to make another set of folds. What do the "rocks" look like now if you slice off the top?

SUPPLIES:

- at least 3 colors of play clay
- butter knife
- rolling pin

PLAY IG, SED, META

Have you ever played rock, paper, scissors? Here's a variation to try with a friend using the rock cycle. Each player should make a fist with one hand and open the other hand flat with palm up. Tap your fist on your palm three times, saying "Ig, Sed, Meta." After the third tap, say "go" and form one of three shapes:

1 **An igneous rock ("Ig")**, with your fingers spread and pointing up—your fingers represent the lava and ash spraying up from a volcano.

2 **A sedimentary rock ("Sed")**, with your hand facing down and parallel with the floor—this represents the flat layers of sediment that are deposited.

3 **A metamorphic rock ("Meta")**, with your thumb and fingers forming an upside-down "V"—this represents a mountain, where many metamorphic rocks are formed.

The winner of each round depends on what type of rock is formed.

+ If Ig and Sed are played, Sed wins, because a sedimentary rock can be made up of eroded igneous rocks.

+ If Sed and Meta are played, Meta wins, because metamorphic rocks can be formed from sedimentary rocks.

+ If Meta and Ig are played, Ig wins, because when metamorphic rocks sink into the mantle, they melt to form magma, which later forms igneous rocks.

If you want to get tricky, reverse things, so that Ig beats Sed, Sed beats Meta, and Meta beats Ig. Why do you think this way is equally correct—geologically speaking, that is?

MAKE MAGIC METAMORPHIC BARS

CAUTION: Ask an adult to help put the pan in and out of the oven!

1 Preheat the oven to 350 degrees Fahrenheit (175 degrees Celsius). Place the butter in the pan and place it in the oven for a few minutes to melt the butter. Meanwhile, wrap the graham crackers in wax paper. Pound the crackers into crumbs.

2 Remove the pan from the oven with a hot pad. Sprinkle about 2 cups of graham cracker crumbs evenly onto the butter, covering every area.

3 Sprinkle a layer of chocolate chips over the graham crackers. Then sprinkle on a layer of each of the following: walnuts, other chips, then coconut flakes. Last, drizzle the sweetened condensed milk evenly over every area of the pan.

4 Place in the oven and bake for about 25 minutes. Take out the bars and let cool completely. Cut into squares. Mmm—yummy rocks!

THINGS TO NOTICE

+ Look at the cut edges of your bars. Do you see layers? Did your layers of ingredients stay the same, or did they change? Did the color or texture or both change?

+ Sometimes in metamorphism fluids (like water with dissolved minerals) help to change the rocks even more. Did you have an ingredient that acted like a fluid?

SUPPLIES:

- O 9-by-13-inch baking pan (23 by 30 centimeters)
- O ½ cup (1 stick) butter
- O wax paper
- O several graham crackers
- O hot pad
- O 12 ounces chocolate chips
- O 2 cups walnut pieces
- O 12 ounces butterscotch chips (or white chocolate or mint)
- O 2 cups coconut flakes or raisins
- O 14 ounces sweetened condensed milk

FOSSILS

Long ago, monstrous animals roamed the earth. Some of them measured over one hundred feet from head to tail. Who were they? Dinosaurs! How do we know so much about them? **FOSSILS!** Fossils are the remains of ancient plants and animals preserved in rock.

Fossils include shells, bones, imprints, tracks, and sometimes even an entire organism, although that is very rare. They don't form every time an organism dies. Lots of steps must happen for a plant or animal to become a fossil that we can then see in a museum.

HOW FOSSILS ARE FORMED

STEP ONE: Most dead plants and animals decay or are eaten. Sometimes, though, the remains are buried quickly enough by sediments that they have a chance to become a fossil.

STEP 2: Usually the soft tissue, like skin, rots away. Water with minerals dissolved in it seeps into tiny pores in the bones and/or shells left behind. Even the soft parts of a plant or animal can be replaced by minerals.

STEP 3: More sediments pile on. The pressure and heat produced by the weight of the sediments evaporates the water and hardens the bones or shells and surrounding sediments into rock. A fossil is born!

STEP 4: Much later, movements in the crust lift up the rock containing the fossil. The rocks above the fossil are eroded by wind, water, and ice, leaving the fossil to be found.

STEP 5: PALEONTOLOGISTS carefully remove the surrounding rock and bring the fossil to a museum. Unearthing fossils and preparing them for removal can take years. Sometimes paleontologists use picks and brushes the size of your toothbrush to prepare fossils as large as school buses!

WORDS 2 KNOW

FOSSIL: the remains of past animal or plant life, preserved in rocks. Fossils include shells, bones, imprints, tracks, and rarely the entire the organism.

PALEONTOLOGIST: a scientist who studies life from long ago.

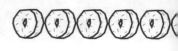

Most fossils are from ocean creatures, especially shellfish. That's because shells and bones are covered by sediments more quickly in the ocean. On land, remains of animals usually rot away before they can be preserved. Almost everything can be a fossil—even poop! Fossilized poop is called **COPROLITE**, and can help paleontologists find out about an animal's diet.

Animals can also be preserved in amber, which is fossilized tree sap. Some pieces of amber contain whole insects trapped in the sap long ago. The ancient Greeks believed amber to be hardened rays of sunlight.

WHY ARE FOSSILS IMPORTANT?

Fossils are important for lots of reasons. They're interesting, of course. It's amazing to hold the fossil of a plant or animal that lived millions of years ago in your hand, or to go to a museum and see the enormous jaws and teeth of a Tyrannosaurus rex! But fossils do two other important things.

COPROLITE: fossilized poop.

INDEX FOSSIL: a fossil from an organism that is known to have lived in a particular time period.

INDEX FOSSILS help tell geologists how old layers of rock are. How? There are some organisms that only lived during limited time periods in the earth's history. These organisms form index fossils.

Herodotus, a historian who lived in ancient Rome during the fourth century BCE, found fossil seashells far inland in Egypt. He suggested that the Mediterranean Sea must once have extended much farther south.

If you find an index fossil in a rock, you know about when the rock was formed. Index fossils have been used to figure out that certain layers of rocks formed at the same time, even if the rocks are nowhere near each other.

Figuring Out the Layers

Born in 1769, William Smith never went to college, but that didn't stop him from making a major contribution to geology. Smith worked as a surveyor, someone who measures the boundaries and elevations of land, all over England. He observed the rocks that he saw very carefully, and noticed that fossils could be found in the same order from top to bottom in sections of rock across England.

William made amazing maps using the information he got from fossils. He made the first geologic map of England, which measured 8 feet (2½ meters) long and 6 feet (2 meters) wide. At first, he didn't get the respect he deserved because he wasn't educated. He even went to debtor's prison because he had difficulty earning money. Later on, however, other geologists honored his discoveries with their highest award, the Wollaston Medal.

What do you get when two Tyrannosaurus rex's crash their cars?

"T" WRECKS!

PALEOECOLOGY is a big word that describes a simple idea. It involves using fossils and rocks to tell us what the environment was like long ago. For example, if fossils from coral reefs are found far to the north, we know that the continent they are on either moved or had a much warmer climate in the past. We also know that the area once existed at the edge of a sea. That's because corals grow in warm, shallow water. Scientists usually use information from different fossils in an area to figure out what the environment was like.

THE BONE WARS

What's big and scaly all over? Dinosaurs! For dinosaurs, big means REALLY big. *Amphicoelias fragillimus* could grow up to 180 feet long (55 meters), more than half the length of a football field. It could weigh up to 122 metric tons, about the weight of 4,370 nine-year-olds put together.

Fossils usually form from the hard parts of animals, like bones and shells. But occasionally, the soft parts are preserved too. Entire woolly mammoths, creatures that lived 10,000 years ago, have been found in the ice in northern Russia. Mammoths are now **EXTINCT**, but were in the same family as elephants.

Dinosaur Body Temperature

Dinosaur bones have been found on every continent, including Antarctica! Many scientists now think that dinosaurs were **WARM-BLOODED**. This means that they kept a steady, warm body temperature. Nearly all other reptiles are **COLD-BLOODED**, which means their temperature changes with their surroundings. Being warm-blooded would have helped dinosaurs live in very cold areas.

People have been finding dinosaur bones for thousands of years. The Chinese thought they came from dragons, and Europeans believed they were left by giant humans. Finally, in the early 1800s, geologists started recognizing and describing dinosaurs. The first dinosaur in the United States was found in 1858 in New Jersey. After that, people went crazy for dinosaur bones. Two paleontologists, Edward Cope and Othniel Marsh, fiercely competed with each other to find bones.

JUST FOR LAUGHS!

What comes after extinction?
Y-TINCTION.

What comes after Y-tinction?
Z-END!

WORDS 2 KNOW

PALEOECOLOGY: the use of fossils and rocks to tell what the environment was like long ago.

EXTINCT: a species that has died out and no longer has any left living.

WARM-BLOODED: an animal that maintains a constant body temperature that doesn't change with its surroundings. Mammals and birds are warm-blooded.

COLD-BLOODED: an animal whose body temperature changes with its surroundings. Reptiles, fish, and insects are cold-blooded.

Their competition was called the "Bone Wars." Cope and Marsh were in such a hurry to find more fossils that they often used dynamite to break open rock where fossils might be. When they left sites where they had found fossils, the two paleontologists buried or destroyed the rocks there so that no one else could find other fossils.

Sally Sells Seashells by the Sea Shore

Try saying that five times fast! The famous tongue twister is actually based on Mary Anning, an early British fossil collector, who was born in 1799 in England. Mary's father died when she was ten, leaving the family in debt, so Mary started hunting for fossils and selling them to keep the family going.

When she was twelve, Mary discovered the first **Ichthyosaurus**, a massive fish-like reptile that weighed up to one ton! Later on, she also found a plesiosaur, another enormous marine reptile. Her work was so important to paleontology that she was made an honorary member of the Geological Society of London.

Petrificus Totalus

You may have heard of the spell in the Harry Potter books that causes the victim's body to freeze up. The idea of "petrifying," or turning to stone, is important to another type of fossil: **PETRIFIED WOOD.** Like bones or shells, wood can also be turned into stone.

There aren't many examples of petrified wood because it's unusual for tree trunks to be quickly covered by sediments and mineral-filled water. But at Petrified Forest National Park in Arizona, there are many giant stone tree trunks from millions of years ago. The petrified wood is almost all quartz, and can only be cut with diamond-tipped saws.

Cope and Marsh spied on each other and bribed each other's workers for information. Once, their crews even got into a rock fight against each other. But both men also made huge strides in understanding the past. Between them, Cope and Marsh discovered 136 new dinosaur species!

JUST FOR LAUGHS!

W hy did the dinosaur cross the road?

BECAUSE THERE WEREN'T ANY CHICKENS YET!

WORDS 2 KNOW

PETRIFIED WOOD: a type of fossil formed from wood that has turned to stone from water filled with minerals.

MAKE YOUR OWN FOSSIL

Note: NEVER pour plaster down the sink.

Try this activity to get an idea of how a fossil forms.

1 Cut off the top of the milk carton so what's left is about 4 inches tall. Spread petroleum jelly on the inside of the carton and on the object you will be making a fossil of.

2 Pour about 2 cups plaster of Paris and 1 cup water into the ziplock bag. Seal the bag and squish the mixture until it is thick and smooth, but you can still pour it. Pour the mixture into the carton.

3 Press the object you want to make a fossil of into the plaster so that one-half is covered by plaster and the rest is exposed. You can use more than one object if they fit. Let it stay there until the plaster starts to become firm. Carefully remove the object and let the plaster continue to dry, at least 30 minutes (this will vary depending on how humid the day is). You now have a plaster cast.

4 Coat the cast and the inside of the carton with petroleum jelly. Mix 1 cup plaster of Paris and ½ cup water, and paprika or food coloring.

SUPPLIES:

- ◌ empty half-gallon cardboard milk carton
- ◌ scissors
- ◌ petroleum jelly
- ◌ water
- ◌ about 3 cups plaster of Paris, from the hardware or craft store
- ◌ large ziplock plastic bag
- ◌ seashell, plastic egg, leaf, or other distinctive shape
- ◌ food coloring or paprika
- ◌ fine sandpaper

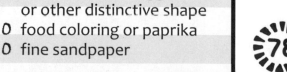

5 Pour the plaster into your cast. You can either pour it in until it just fills the impression of each object, or you can pour in all of the plaster so that it's an inch or more thick. Let it dry thoroughly, about 2 hours or overnight. This is a plaster mold.

6 Carefully remove the mold from the cast. You can make more molds if you like. When you're done, you can use fine sandpaper to smooth the surface, and paint your mold if you like.

THINGS TO NOTICE

+ When you press the object into the wet plaster, it's like the first step in a real fossil being made. What kinds of real substances are like plaster?

+ Do you think it would take more or less time for a real fossil to form than it took you?

+ What other kinds of objects would make good fossils? Why?

You can also use this method to make casts and molds of animal tracks that you find. In this case, you would cut off the bottom of the milk carton, and press the milk carton (now open at both ends) into the soil around the track. Pour the plaster in and let it dry.

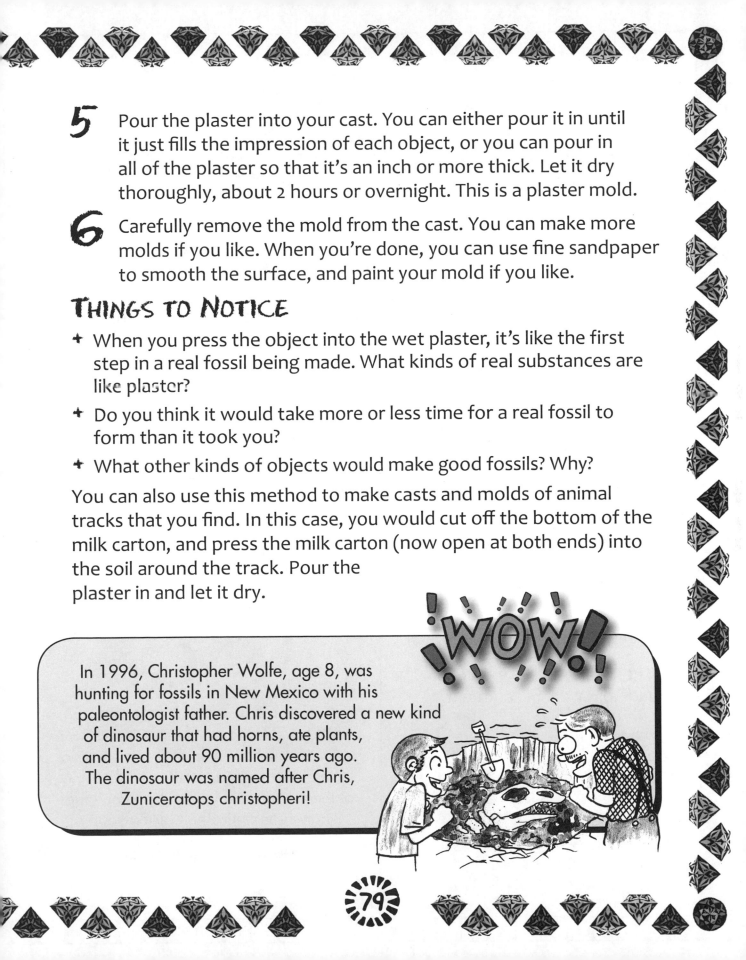

In 1996, Christopher Wolfe, age 8, was hunting for fossils in New Mexico with his paleontologist father. Chris discovered a new kind of dinosaur that had horns, ate plants, and lived about 90 million years ago. The dinosaur was named after Chris, Zuniceratops christopheri!

TAKE A WALK THROUGH TIME

The earth is incredibly old. Compared with the age of the earth, humans have only lived for a very short period of time. Try this activity to get some idea of how long rocks and creatures have been around.

Grab a friend or adult who's good at counting. Pick a place where you can walk for 10 minutes or so without stopping, like a walking path or your school playground. Start walking and count out loud together for every step you take. When you get to the steps listed below, say the step first, then what happened in that "step," listed in bold. Then keep walking and counting. Each step you take represents 10 million years.

STROMATOLITES: fossils made of layers of sediment built up by blue-green bacteria.

WORDS 2 KNOW

The oldest known fossils are **STROMATOLITES**. These are layers of sediment built up by blue-green bacteria. Scientists disagree about how old some of them are, but think they may be older than three and a half billion years.

Step 1	**Earth formed** (4.6 billion years ago)
Step 57	**Oldest Rocks** (4.03 billion years ago)
Step 90	**Oldest Fossils** (3.79 billion years ago)
Step 405	**First Abundant Life** (545 million years ago)
Step 407	**First Fish** (530 million years ago)
Step 437	**First Dinosaurs** (248 million years ago)
Step 454	**Dinosaurs Extinct** (65 million years ago)
Step 455	**First Dogs** (54 million years ago)
Step 458	**First Horses** (23 million years ago)
Step 459 ½	**First Human Ancestors** (5.5 million years ago)
Step 460	**First Humans** (160,000 years ago)
Step 460	**Present Day**

THINGS TO NOTICE

✦ Whew! That was a lot of walking, and humans only came into the picture at the very, very end of your walk.

Dinosaur National Monument

Dinosaur National Monument in Colorado and Utah has fossils from over one billion years ago. But it's especially known for its dinosaurs. The Visitor Center has a spectacular display of over 1,600 dinosaur fossil bones left in the original rock. So far, 11 different species of dinosaurs have been discovered at Dinosaur National Monument.

BECOME A ROCKHOUND

Anybody can become a ROCKHOUND, including you! Even if you live in the city, you can still collect rocks. You might have already begun a collection, if you've picked up some especially pretty or interesting rocks and brought them home.

Rocks exist all around you. Some lie in their natural surroundings, while others have been used to make other things. When you collect rocks, always practice safe behavior and use the rules listed here.

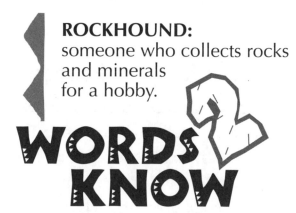

ROCKHOUND: someone who collects rocks and minerals for a hobby.

WORDS 2 KNOW

Safety Rules for Collecting

Here are some rules to follow so you stay safe when collecting rocks and minerals.

- Take an adult with you if you go outside your own back yard.

- Ask permission before you enter someone else's property.

- Collect rocks at a safe distance from the road. Stay away from rock overhangs.

- **NEVER** go into old mines or rock quarries, because they're dangerous! Plus, the most interesting rocks there have probably been removed already.

- Don't collect rocks from national parks or monuments. This is illegal!

- **ALWAYS** use a rock hammer to hit rocks, because a regular hammer could break and injure you in the process.

- **ALWAYS** wear safety goggles when you hit rocks with a hammer.

- Wear sturdy shoes or boots and long pants. If you're working near an overhang where rocks could fall, wear a safety helmet.

COLLECTING ROCKS & MINERALS

When you find a rock to add to your collection, wrap it in a piece of newspaper, and put a number on the newspaper. Record important information about the rock in a small notebook—where you discovered it, the date, and a brief description. You might want to take a picture or make a sketch of where you found it, as well as any other interesting features in the area. When you get home, transfer the number from the newspaper to a small label, and put it on the rock, so you don't lose track of what it is.

PLACES TO FIND ROCKS

There are two types of places to find rocks. One is a rock outcrop, such as in cliffs or places where rocks jut up from the ground. Rocks in outcrops are part of the bedrock under the soil, and not just a boulder or rock fragment. The second type is where rock fragments have been deposited from somewhere else, such as streams or beaches. When you are collecting rocks from streambeds or beaches, you might think about where the rocks originally came from and how they reached their current location. Here are other places to look:

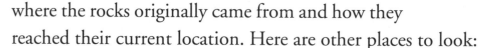

- ❀ Your driveway, back yard, or schoolyard
- ❀ Hills and mountains
- ❀ Beaches, especially rocky seashores
- ❀ Roadsides (stay a safe distance from cars!)
- ❀ Special collecting areas (you can find these in geology guidebooks for your area)
- ❀ Rock and gem shows
- ❀ Stores specializing in rocks and gems
- ❀ Natural history museums

Best of all, find a buddy who wants to collect rocks and minerals. You can hunt for rocks together, and then trade them with each other or other rock-collecting friends.

Equipment for Rock Hunting

You can start collecting rocks in your backyard without any special equipment at all. As you get more interested in rock collecting, you may want to seek out some useful tools. You can find most of these at a hardware store.

- Rock hammer. Rock hammers are different from regular hammers because they are made out of special, extra-strong steel. This makes them safer to use.

- Safety eye goggles. You should wear goggles whenever you use a hammer to hit a rock.

- Hand lens or magnifying glass, to see crystals within rocks.

- Sturdy backpack to carry rocks, equipment, food, and water.

- Pieces of newspaper or plastic bags, to hold your rocks.

- Map and compass, so you can find your way around new sites.

- Camera, to take pictures of collection sites (optional).

- Notebook and pencil or pen.

- First aid kit, just in case.

IDENTIFYING ROCKS AND MINERALS

You may want to collect rocks based simply on their appearance. However, you might also want to try to figure out what kinds of rocks you have found. Don't worry if you can't tell what your rocks are yet. It can be tricky, even for experienced geologists. Here are some tips to find out what kinds of rocks you have collected.

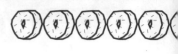

WHERE DID YOU FIND YOUR ROCK? Location is very important. The geology of your area can tell you a lot about what kinds of rocks you might find. If you live in the mountains, you may find metamorphic rocks. If there are volcanoes near you, you may discover igneous rocks. If you live on the Plains, you may find sedimentary rocks, like limestone.

WHAT MINERALS ARE IN YOUR ROCK? Look very closely at it. Use a mineral identification book from the library with pictures of and information about minerals in order to identify them. You can also refer to the descriptions in chapter 2.

IS YOUR ROCK IGNEOUS, SEDIMENTARY, OR METAMORPHIC? If it has layers in it, it is probably either sedimentary or metamorphic. Shiny bits of mica suggest it's metamorphic, while grains of sand indicate it's sedimentary. If it's dull gray in color, earthy, and/or has fossils in it, it may be limestone. If the rock has intergrown crystals and no layers, it's probably igneous.

Most likely, you'll find a relatively common type of rock. While quartz and diamonds are both clear and shiny, diamonds are rare. So if you find a rock like this in your backyard, it's probably quartz, the most common mineral present in the earth's crust! Check out the descriptions of common rocks in chapters 3–5.

JUST FOR LAUGHS!

What kind of dog loves rocks?
A ROCKHOUND!

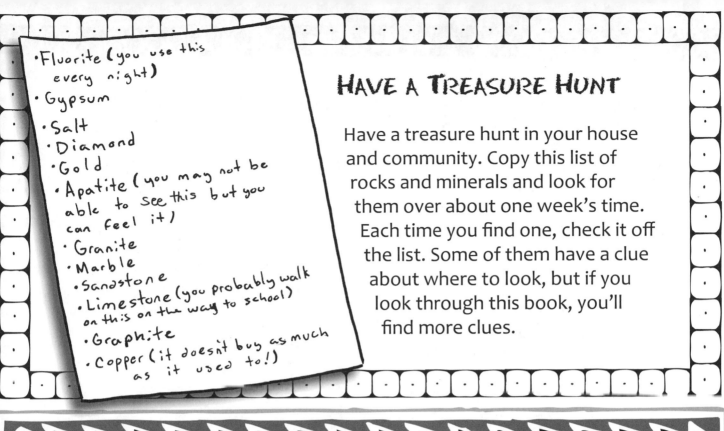

- Fluorite (you use this every night)
- Gypsum
- Salt
- Diamond
- Gold
- Apatite (you may not be able to see this but you can feel it)
- Granite
- Marble
- Sandstone
- Limestone (you probably walk on this on the way to school)
- Graphite
- Copper (it doesn't buy as much as it used to!)

HAVE A TREASURE HUNT

Have a treasure hunt in your house and community. Copy this list of rocks and minerals and look for them over about one week's time. Each time you find one, check it off the list. Some of them have a clue about where to look, but if you look through this book, you'll find more clues.

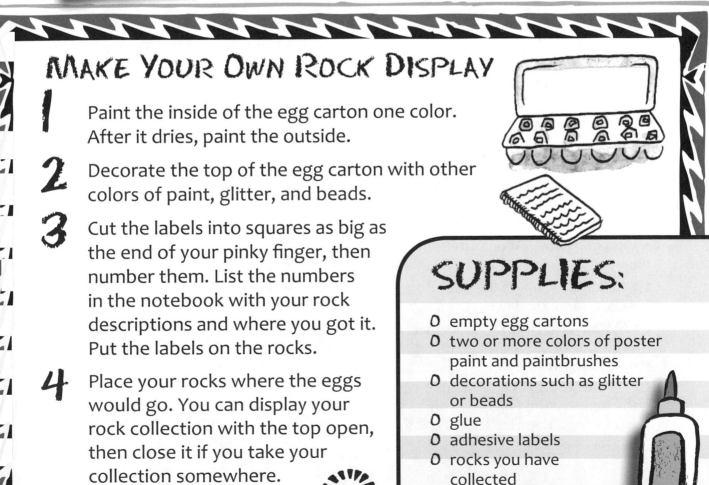

MAKE YOUR OWN ROCK DISPLAY

1 Paint the inside of the egg carton one color. After it dries, paint the outside.

2 Decorate the top of the egg carton with other colors of paint, glitter, and beads.

3 Cut the labels into squares as big as the end of your pinky finger, then number them. List the numbers in the notebook with your rock descriptions and where you got it. Put the labels on the rocks.

4 Place your rocks where the eggs would go. You can display your rock collection with the top open, then close it if you take your collection somewhere.

SUPPLIES:

- O empty egg cartons
- O two or more colors of poster paint and paintbrushes
- O decorations such as glitter or beads
- O glue
- O adhesive labels
- O rocks you have collected
- O pen

ACIDIC: acids are chemicals that taste sour. Examples are vinegar, lemon juice, and acids in your stomach.

ASH: rock and glass fragments that are smaller than a pinhead, produced from an explosive volcano.

ATMOSPHERE: the gases that surround the earth.

ATOMS: the smallest particles that cannot be easily broken down.

BEDS: layers of sedimentary rocks.

BLACK SMOKERS: a sea vent that spews black smoke and very hot water with sulfur.

CARAT: a measure of weight for gems equal to 200 milligrams.

CARBON: a type of atom that is present in all life. It is what the minerals diamond and graphite are made of.

CHEMICAL SEDIMENTARY ROCK: sedimentary rock that forms when water that contains dissolved minerals evaporates and leaves behind the mineral deposits.

CHLORINE: a type of atom that combines with sodium to form salt.

CLASTIC SEDIMENTARY ROCKS: sedimentary rocks that form from rock fragments, or clasts, pressed together.

CLASTS: rock fragments such as pebbles, sand, or clay.

COARSE-GRAINED: rocks that have mineral grains that are large enough to see with just your eyes.

COLD-BLOODED: an animal whose body temperature changes with its surroundings. Reptiles, fish, and insects are cold-blooded.

COMPASS: an instrument used for navigation, with a needle that always points north.

CONTACT METAMORPHISM: metamorphism that happens when rocks come into contact with hot magma.

CONTINENTAL CRUST: the part of the earth's crust that forms the continents.

CONTINENTAL DRIFT: the theory that all of the continents were joined together at one time and have since moved apart.

COPROLITE: fossilized poop.

CORE: the center layer of the earth composed of iron and nickel. It has two parts: a solid inner core, and a liquid outer core.

CRUST: the thin, hard, outer layer of the earth.

CRYSTAL: a solid with a definite geometric shape. Crystals have edges and smooth flat areas called faces. Crystals are made of atoms arranged in a pattern.

CRYSTALLINE: any material that has atoms arranged in a pattern that repeats itself. Minerals are crystalline materials.

DENSER: more matter in the same amount of space.

DEPOSIT: leave behind. For example, muddy water can deposit mud as it flows over a surface or evaporates.

DIKES: a sheet of igneous rock that cuts across other rocks.

EARTHQUAKE: a shaking of the earth's crust because of movement in the earth's plates or because of a volcano's activity.

EQUATOR: the imaginary line dividing the north and south halves of the earth.

EROSION: the process where rocks are broken down by wind, water, ice, and gravity, and then carried away.

EVAPORATE: when a liquid turns into a gas.

EVAPORITE: a mineral that forms by the evaporation of seawater, leaving dissolved minerals behind. Examples are salt and gypsum.

EXTINCT: a species that has died out and no longer has any left living.

EXTRUSIVE IGNEOUS ROCKS: rocks that form from lava cooling and becoming solid on the surface of the earth.

FACET: a smooth, flat, cut or polished side of a gemstone.

FINE-GRAINED: rocks that have mineral grains that are too small to see with just your eyes.

FOLIATION: flat layers within metamorphic rocks. The layers form as minerals grow under pressure.

FOSSIL: the remains of past animal or plant life, preserved in rocks. Fossils include shells, bones, imprints, tracks, and rarely the entire the organism.

GEMSTONE: a cut or polished mineral that is beautiful, durable, and rare.

GEOLOGISTS: scientists who study the rocks, minerals, and physical structure of an area.

HABIT: the shape that a crystal tends to grow in.

HEXAGON: a shape with six sides.

HIMALAYAS: a mountain chain between India and Tibet. It contains the world's highest mountain, Mount Everest, which is 29,029 feet (8,848 meters) above sea level.

IGNEOUS ROCKS: rocks that form from cooling magma.

INDEX FOSSIL: a fossil from an organism that is known to have lived in a particular time period.

INTRUSIVE IGNEOUS ROCKS: rocks that form from magma cooling and becoming solid below the surface of the earth.

LAVA: magma that comes to the surface of the earth.

MAGMA: molten rock.

MAGNET: a substance that attracts iron and produces a magnetic field.

MAGNETIC FIELD: a field of force produced by a magnetic object.

MANTLE: the middle layer of the earth. Some areas of the mantle have melted rocks. It is soft enough that the rocks flow very slowly.

METAMORPHIC ROCKS: rocks that have been transformed by heat or pressure or both into new rocks, while staying solid.

METAMORPHOSE: to completely change something's nature or appearance.

METEORITE: a piece of rock that has entered the earth's atmosphere.

MINERALS: naturally occurring solids that almost always have a crystalline structure. Rocks are made of minerals.

MUDFLOW: a high-speed flow of mud formed from lava and ash mixing with melted snow and rain.

OCEANIC CRUST: the earth's crust under the oceans.

ORGANIC SEDIMENTARY ROCKS: sedimentary rocks that form from the remains of plants or animals.

OXYGEN: the most abundant element in the earth's crust. Found in air, water, and many rocks.

PALEOECOLOGY: the use of fossils and rocks to tell what the environment was like long ago.

PALEONTOLOGIST: a scientist who studies life from long ago.

PARENT ROCK: the original rock from which another rock was formed.

PETRIFIED WOOD: a type of fossil formed from wood that has turned to stone from water filled with minerals.

PLATE TECTONICS: the theory that describes how the plates move across the earth and interact with each other to produce earthquakes, volcanoes, and mountains.

PLATES: huge, interconnected slabs of the earth's crust that slowly move.

PRESSURE: the force applied to something.

RECRYSTALLIZATION: during metamorphism, when atoms in the minerals pack closer together to form new crystals because of greater pressures and heat.

REGIONAL METAMORPHISM: metamorphism that happens over large regions, usually forming long mountain chains.

ROCKHOUND: someone who collects rocks and minerals for a hobby.

ROCKS: solid natural substances that are made up of minerals.

SEDIMENTARY ROCKS: rocks formed from sediments, the remains of plants or animals, or from the evaporation of seawater.

SEDIMENTS: small particles of rocks or minerals, such as clay, sand, or pebbles.

SILICON: the next most abundant element in the earth's crust. Found in sand, clay, and quartz.

SODIUM: a type of atom that combines with chlorine to form salt.

SOLUTION: a fluid with a substance dissolved in it. Salt water is a solution.

STALACTITE: a cave formation that looks like an icicle hanging from the ceiling.

STALAGMITE: a cave formation projecting up from the floor, often underneath a stalactite.

STROMATOLITES: fossils made of layers of sediment built up by blue-green bacteria.

SUBSTANCE: a kind of matter or material.

TEXTURE: the size, shape, and arrangement of grains or crystals in a rock.

UNIVERSE: everything that exists, everywhere.

VOLCANO: an opening in the earth's crust. Magma, ash, and gases erupt out of volcanos.

WARM-BLOODED: an animal that maintains a constant body temperature that doesn't change with its surroundings. Mammals and birds are warm-blooded.

BOOKS

Anderson, Alan, Gwen Diehn, and Terry Krautwurst. *Geology Crafts for Kids: 50 Nifty Projects to Explore the Marvels of Planet Earth.* New York: Sterling, 1998.

Blobaum, Cindy and Michael Kline. *Geology Rocks!: 50 Hands-On Activities to Explore the Earth.* Vermont: Williamson Publishing Company, 1999.

Bonewitz, Ronald Louis. *Rock and Gem.* New York: DK Smithsonian, 2008.

Farndon, John. *The Complete Guide to Rocks & Minerals.* Massachusetts: World Publications Group, 2007.

Farndon, John. *How the Earth Works.* New York: Dorling Kindersley Publishers Ltd, 1999.

Pough, Frederick H. *Peterson First Guide to Rocks and Minerals.* New York: Houghton Mifflin Company, 1991.

Symes, R.F. and R.R Harding. *Crystal and Gem.* New York: DK Children, 2007.

Symes, R. F. *Rocks & Minerals.* New York: DK Children, 2008

Van Rose, Susanna and Anita Ganeri. *The Big Atlas of the Earth & Sea.* New York: DK Publishing, 1999.

Ward, David. *Fossils (Smithsonian Handbooks).* DK Adult, 2002.

WEB SITES

U.S. Geological Survey (U.S.G.S.) http://geomaps.wr.usgs.gov/parks/rxmin/index.html

U.S.G.S. Earthquakes for Kids http://earthquake.usgs.gov/learn/kids/

U.S.G.S. in your schoolyard! http://education.usgs.gov/schoolyard/

National Park Service http://www.nps.gov/

The City Rocks! Explore the Hidden World of Building Stone http://homepage.mac.com/ebandpck/cityrocks/intro.html

The story of the Haddonfield "Bone Wars" www.levins.com/dinosaur.shtml

Strange Science: The Rocky Road to Modern Paleontology and Biology www.strangescience.net/

Extreme Science www.extremescience.com/

Enchanted Learning www.enchantedlearning.com

Science News for Kids www.sciencenewsforkids.org

The Story of the Hope Diamond at the Smithsonian http://mineralsciences.si.edu/hope.htm

Mineral Information Institute www.mii.ort/commonminerals.html

MUSEUMS

Smithsonian National Museum of Natural History, Washington, D.C. www.mnh.si.edu/earth

University of California Museum of Paleontology www.ucmp.berkeley.edu/

Philadelphia Academy of Natural Sciences www.ansp.org/

Carnegie Museum of Natural History, Pittsburgh, PA www.carnegiemnh.org/

Mineralogical Museum at Harvard University, Cambridge, MA www.fas.harvard.edu/~geomus/minerals/htm

Yale University Peabody Museum of Natural History www.peabody.yale.edu/

Franklin Mineral Museum, Franklin, NJ www.darron.net/franklinmineralmuseum/

The Burke Museum of Natural History and Culture, Seattle, WA www.washington.edu/burkemuseum/kids/index.php

Arizona Mining and Mineral Museum, Phoenix, AZ www.admmr.state.za.us

The Mineral Museum of Michigan www.museum.mtu.edu//

The Field Museum, Chicago, IL www.fieldmuseum.org/

Mineral and Fossil Museums, Exhibits, and Displays in the USA www.osomin.com/exhibit.htm